Come See Matt LIVE!

Join Matt for **his world-famous Success Revolution seminar!** In this *breakthrough weekend experience,* watch as life transforms before your eyes! Matt will take you through **creating the life you deserve now,** and help you **step into the future of your dreams!**

Receive up to *2 FREE tickets*
Value of $1590!

Transform your life today and reserve early.
Seating is extremely limited!

Read More and Register at:
www.successrevolutionlive.com

(Must register online to redeem your FREE tickets)

Free DVD Valued at $97

In this brand-new DVD, Matt Brauning takes you through the **3 Keys to Unleash Ultimate Success**. Watch, and learn how to create the life of your dreams, and truly

MASTER YOUR LIFE

Order from the website to have the
Free DVD valued at $97 shipped to your home
Or watch online right now!

Order at:
www.AddictedToNothing.com

Download the *E-Book, FREE!*

Please help me share this message! **I am GIVING away the ebook!** If someone you know needs to read this book, Please share it with them now!

Give *Total Freedom From Addictions*
As an ***E-Book*** *for* **FREE!**

Go to:

www.addictedtonothing.com

TOTAL FREEDOM FROM ADDICTIONS

Jade,
Thank you for
Changing TheWorld!

MATT BRAUNING

MNLP MTD MHT

For information on this book,
To download the **FREE E-Book** to share,
And to order the **FREE DVD**
visit www.addictedtonothing.com

For more information on eliminating addictions,
personal coaching, seminars, or trainings, please
visit the author's website at:
www.evolutionseminars.com
Or call toll free: (888) 212-5744

You may contact the author with any comments,
questions, or testimonials at:
Answers@addictedtonothing.com

DEDICATION

This book is dedicated to my mother, Linda, and my father, Rick. Thank you both for everything you have taught, shown, and helped me to understand. I am more appreciative than you will ever know.

NEW EDITION PREFACE

When this book was first published in 2007, I had recently ended my own addictive behavior. I kept falling into that old quit-relapse-quit cycle. At first, I wrote this book really just intending it as an answer for drug addicts and alcoholics. By the time I finished it, though, I realized that other people fight this battle every day, and they do it with more behaviors and substances than one could ever acknowledge.

My journey has taken me from the depths of despair to the certainty of AA, to a post-AA life, to the confidence that comes with great success as an entrepreneur and speaker. It's this last part of my life that has given me the most tools for change, for compassion, and for understanding of just how incredibly common the stress of addiction actually is.

As I taught the skills of making rapid change at high schools, colleges, and professional business trainings, I began to see people struggling with everyday addictions like sugar, love, cigarettes, food, biting nails, sleeping in, procrastination, shopping, hoarding, and so much more. It seemed that everywhere I looked, someone was struggling with something. As I really started using the rapid-change skills of NLP, Hypnosis, Time Dynamics, and Coaching, I helped end all kinds of addictions for clients all over the world.

One client in Melbourne, Australia couldn't quit smoking, no matter what, until he met me. We had a 30-minute conversation and he literally quit on the spot. Another teenager in Orange County kept biting her nails, and with one session she dropped the habit. Breaking through the wall of addiction just gets easier and easier, and that's what prompted me to write this new edition.

ORIGINAL PREFACE

My intention for this book is to answer questions that might help further readers' personal growth and help them through a journey I recently went through myself. It is meant to foster understanding of why we do what we do and, in the process, give some answers about 12-Step Programs and addiction. Please do not confuse it as "the new way," "the new religion," or "the answer." It is none of those things. There are plenty of books out now that will tell you "how to get sober without AA," or how to stay "clean for good." This book does not aspire to any of those claims.

Many of the people who helped me with ideas for this book are so-called "anti-AA," while some just found other ways to fill their needs. There are many documents out there, mostly available on the Internet, regarding anti-AA sentiments and anti-step work ideas. It is very important to me not to be classified in that genre.

Rather this book represents an attempt to share only what I have learned personally through psychology, self-improvement, the programs, spiritual growth, and life's experience in the hope that you may find it useful in your life, especially if you currently are at a crossroads. My opinions on whether AA is bad or good are not relevant; therefore, I will not talk about them here. Maybe one day if I am bored enough I will begin a chartroom or start a blog or something like that on AA. However, that is highly unlikely.

Please take from this text what you can use for your own personal growth and leave the rest.

Thank you very much and, from my heart, enjoy.

CONTENTS

PART 1

WHAT'S THIS ALL ABOUT?

CHAPTER 1
READY FOR A JOURNEY

I still remember the day I moved away from home. We all did it a different way, but we all had something in common. None of us knew what was coming. I can even remember saying to myself, "You don't know what you're supposed to do now." I felt like the future wasn't mine; it was totally uncertain, almost frightening. But I had already left my old home, and had to start something new. Now, I had no idea what this "something new" was going to be, and I wasn't even sure I wanted it, whatever it was! But it's time to move forward. Sure, I could try and beg my way back to my old home, where life felt certain. But, then what? As scary as it was, all I could tell myself was, "It's time to grow."

So I moved past some of the uncertainty, and I scrounged up enough money (with two friends) to rent my first apartment. I was 19. It was all so new, because I never before felt like, you know, you're the one in control. It was near the end of the year, and my birthday was coming up.

When I got home from work, there was a package waiting for me on the doorstep. I hadn't received a package at my new home before! I took it with me as I went inside. Right there in my hands, I had something very exciting. There was a card on top from a close friend, and it said, cryptically:

In your hands is a gift.

It also said that I couldn't open it until my birthday, which was a week away! I wanted to know so badly what this gift was all about; I wanted to look inside the box. Every day I'd come home, pick it up and shake it, just to make sure that it wasn't clothes or something. You know, you always want to make sure that this is something you want.

The days passed like years. I was getting so intensely curious; I knew it must be something really great. If only I could look inside, behind all of the wrapping! You know that feeling, when you just *have* to find out what the gift you're about to open is all about!

It's like getting your first car. All that planning, all that uncertainty, and then finally the day comes, and you're ready to move! Such a sense of freedom, of pure excitement. It's like knowing, for the first time, that you get to choose what's next. When I got mine, I wanted to drive everywhere! I remember walking right up to my brand new, used, run-down sports car, thinking, "With this, anything is possible."

Then I went for the first ride totally by myself, in my very own car. I realized that I could go anywhere I wanted, the choice was mine. So there I was, out on the open road, wind in my hair, my heart pumping, just feeling free now. Yet, I still didn't know where I was going to go. Endless possibilities...

As the winds of change blew through my hair, I started thinking about these old books called *Choose your own Adventure*. I don't know if you remember those, but I read those back in grade school. They were special because at the end of each chapter, the book asks that you choose what happens next. "If you want your hero to steal all the gold, go to page 43. If you want your hero to kill the dragon, go to page 94." The neatest part for me is that there are countless ways any story can turn out. Just when the character in the book gets to a major problem or tragedy, and nothing's going their way, all you need to do is start a new chapter. And, of course, that's when everything changes. Now the character is on his way to great things, to finally winning after it once seemed impossible!

I read a book about a man who broke the marathon record once, and ever since then I wanted to run a marathon. I dreamed about it for years, but it was one of those goals I never really thought I could do. Until one year, I decided to just do it.

The funny thing was, the first part seemed kind of easy, like I just show up, and the marathon seems to run itself for a while. I really thought to myself, "You can totally do this!" Then I looked at the mile marker...and I was only halfway there.

Maybe looking was my mistake, or maybe I just hit my wall at that point—either way, my body was quite upset with me. It didn't know what the hell was going on! By then, I was really struggling, and starting to feel like it just wasn't worth it. It can get really hard after a little while. Then I saw this big banner that changed the rest of the race for me. It read:

After Mile 20, it's no longer the body.
It's the heart of the runner that finishes the race.

That really struck a chord, and I got back in the game. It still hurt, it was still difficult, but now my heart took the lead, and it was going to finish! I ran/walked/hobbled until there were just a couple of miles left. Then I took off.

I ran when I didn't want to. I ran with everything I didn't have left anymore. I ran when all I wanted to do was give up. Like Forrest Gump, I just ran. I passed all these people who'd been leading me the whole time, and they looked at me with shock and disbelief. Minutes later, it's already mile 26. Only .2 miles left. Is that the finish line there in the distance? I sprinted even faster and more determined. It's time to do this...

CHAPTER 2
TOTAL FREEDOM

Ad-dict-ed | Adjective /ə diktid/

1. Physically and mentally dependent on a particular substance
2. Enthusiastically devoted to a particular thing

I've been addicted to all kinds of things. In high school, I was using every day, and drinking afterward. I've been one of those Starbucks-every-day people, and I've been obsessed with eating, too.

I've also been addicted to exercise and health food, if you can believe that! Sure, the end result wasn't the same—I certainly stayed healthier this way—but they still severely limited my choices. I was *compelled* to do them, rather than choosing each time that this is what I wanted to do. That's the very definition of a compulsion, which is why the symptoms of an addiction align with the symptoms of obsessive-compulsive disorder.

Anyone who has attended an AA meeting has heard the warnings about trying to "drink like a gentleman." Basically, to succeed in AA, a person needs to believe that the "alcoholic" gene we have doesn't permit us to tolerate *any* alcohol. But, if alcohol is the culprit, then why is it that, when you take away alcohol from an alcoholic, they often replace the addiction with something else?

As soon as I realized that *anything* could be an addiction, I understood that there may actually be no such thing as an "addiction" in the first place. After six amazing years in AA, I've moved on from the "addiction" mindset and am in an even better place now. Let me explain.

I'm not much for extremes. I don't believe in the all-or-nothing mentality, where you're either a drunk or totally sober, totally clean or off the wagon. I know plenty of people who comfortably fall somewhere in between, so why can't I? After all, our DNA is 99.99% the same, our brains and bodies are made out of the same materials and chemicals, and we all need the same things.

Besides, some addictive behaviors (such as eating, shopping, and even sex) are a part of everyday life, and it would be incredibly unhealthy for a person to have to stop eating, shopping, or having sex altogether for the rest of their life!

So, for me, having total freedom from addictions isn't just about being sober. It's about having *total choice:* the ability to choose what I want to do, when I want to do it. If I want a drink, I want to be able to have a drink. And then I want to be able to stop.

But is this even possible? If you asked me while I was in AA, I could have sworn it wasn't. But if you ask me nowadays, I'll say that I'm living proof that it's not only possible, *it's easy.*

LIVING SOCIAL

Like I said, I used to be incredibly "addicted" to coffee. I had a latte every single day! But now, I can take it or leave it. Most of the time, I choose to leave it, but every once in a while, I have a cup of coffee if I'm out with somebody. That's freedom.

And, just like coffee, I can take alcohol or leave it. Most often I choose not to; sometimes, I do. That may seem like a "lie" or an "impossibility" to those people who've identified themselves deeply as an alcoholic, but I assure you, it's true. It used to be an all-or-nothing thing, but now I'm just a social drinker. This is *total* freedom.

It's not about finding a way to *force* yourself. Saying "don't drink, don't drink, and don't drink, no matter what!" is one of the most difficult decisions to stick to. Having total freedom from addictions is about making old behaviors or old substances into non-issues.

As a consequence of this change in thinking, when I see something like a cigarette it doesn't appeal to me whatsoever. As a matter of fact, it actually leaves me feeling somewhat disgusted. But it's still a non-issue! I don't have to struggle to stay away from it; it's just not part of my life. That's what I hope to achieve for many of you reading this book. If there's something that is really harmful for you that you're still indulging in, I hope it will become a non-issue for you once you understand and apply the tools described in this book.

Now, there are certain things I choose never to indulge in, like any kind of hard drugs or any kind of smoking. For me, that doesn't work at all. With the techniques I'll explain later, I've actually changed my neural pathways around in a way that makes those options completely unappealing to me. So much so, in fact, that I made a decision that I will not invite it into my life. I am not worried that if I use something, I will start back again. I just think, "Why in the World would I ever use drugs?" It just doesn't fit into my life, in any way.

Just to be totally clear, I believe in AA's intentions, and in their basic premise: to find an answer for what they call alcoholism. But the numbers regarding the program's success rate are astounding: *95% of all 12-step participants have relapsed at some point.* As you'll see as you read on, this statistic is not at all surprising, given the makeup of the program. What surprises me is the simple fact that the program stubbornly continues on doing exactly what didn't help those 95% of people!

What the program excels at, though, is creating a safe space for the beginnings of a turnaround. Indeed, my first few years with AA were *incredibly* important in helping me turn my life around. I simply question the sustainability of the results. The unfortunate truth is that most members end up attending meetings for years, while indulging in addictions to smoking, coffee, sugar, sex, or gambling. Sure, some go through their lives and never drink again, but how many truly live? How many are truly free?

Originated in the 1970s by Richard Bandler and John Grinder (a psychologist and a linguist respectively), Neuro-Linguistic Programming (NLP) is what I consider my most powerful tool. After years and years of researching and duplicating patterns in the human brain, Bandler & Grinder were able to compile their findings into a well-organized, entirely new field of thought, complete with full exercises and plenty of new theories. Since then, numerous studies have validated Bandler & Grinder's discoveries. Pick up any books on NLP like *The Structure of Magic Volume I or II, Frogs into Princes, NLP for Dummies, or NLP Magic Demystified,* and you'll blow your mind as you discover how our brains really work.

One of the central tenets of NLP is a phrase that goes, "The map is not the territory." When we look at a map, it doesn't really contain the street we are seeking, but simply a line drawn on a piece of paper to *represent* the territory. In the same way, our minds interpret external stimuli through mental pictures. The difference is that those pictures *do* sometimes feel real to us. It feels real when we see a person doing something to harm us. It feels real when we see a person doing something wonderful for us. And then we act as if they were real.

However, those feelings are just a map. The pictures we create in our minds through our five senses give us perceptions of how to interpret others' actions. While we say a person inflicted pain or pleasure on us, the way that person actually behaved may or may not have had that intention. The action could have been intended to mean something entirely different! The way we *perceive* the action depends on how our minds have filtered the information coming at us; this filtering is based on our needs, beliefs, identities, memories, emotions, values, and even our personality traits!

This is true for the case of drugs, alcohol, or other addictions; we act based on our perception of the addiction, which comes from what we need, believe, identify with, and have acted over time. Thus, when confronted with the substance, it sends us back to a certain place in our unconscious and we get a feeling. When we see a drug, food, or a bottle of alcohol, it triggers a certain response, dictated by our past.

Unfortunately, the "science" of psychology is still much more of an art. There does not exist any one-size-fits-all guide to life. But what I've collected during my life is a group of truths, which when put together paint a vivid picture of why we do the things we do, and when taken as a whole, give a road map toward mastering life, toward total freedom from any addiction.

In my studies with NLP, Hypnotherapy, Time Dynamics, Emotional Freedom Techniques, Reiki, and all sorts of other modalities, there is a recurring theme: The emotional state we have at any given time is made up of two things: our Internal Representation (the way in which we perceive the world) and our Physiology (our breathing, our body, and our biochemistry). Both of these are deeply affected by an addiction, especially when it involves a mood-altering substance or activity. Drugs, alcohol, and even sugar change the way in which we see the world, and affect our biochemistry at the molecular level.

Luckily, these fields of study have a lot to say about taking back control of your mind and body, and getting out from under the grip of addiction.

So what are these truths? What is it that we are supposed to do?

Read on.

CHAPTER 3
YOUR UNCONSCIOUS

What's your phone number?

Got it? Now, where did that number come from? Have you been thinking of it all day, just repeating it over and over in your head in case I asked? Or was it stored somewhere deep within you, where you have access when you need it but can otherwise forget about?

Throughout history, philosophers and psychologists have known, intellectually, that we humans have multiple components of our consciousness. They've described these different aspects of our being using a variety of names: the id, the ego, the superego, the higher self, the inner self, the child self, the subconscious, the unconscious, the superconscious, and many, many more. For the purpose of this book, we'll keep it simple, and just stick with calling it your Unconscious Mind.

We use this terminology in order to make sure we remember the difference between that and our Conscious Mind, the aspect of us that distinguishes between reality and fantasy. That's the part that critiques and judges the world around us. Whenever we think "consciously" about something, we're using—naturally—our Conscious Minds.

The Unconscious, on the other hand, is the part of your mind that you don't normally think about. It is the part that tells your body to breathe you while you sleep, and tells your heart to beat around the clock. This is also the part of the mind that stores our memories, emotions, and other data—like phone numbers.

SERVE AND PROTECT

A *Prime Directive* is a need of the Unconscious Mind that takes primary importance above all else. There are several prime directives, but we'll only cover a couple here.

One important Prime Directive of your Unconscious Mind is to *be your servant*. As a servant, it takes and follows orders. In this respect, we can think of it like a computer, programmed by you and outside influences to perform certain actions and work in certain ways. Throughout our lives, our Unconscious Minds get programmed by the influence of our role models. From birth to age 7, it gets programmed mainly by our parents—whatever they believe, we'll believe, and whatever they do, we want to do. As time passes, our role models become our friends and family, our colleagues and idols, and, eventually, our own experiences. Like a computer, once it is programmed, our Unconscious follows through with the program. If we program our Unconscious so that when some event happens, negative emotions occur, then every time that event happens, we'll have the same feelings.

In the same way, your Unconscious is programmed to prove you right as much as possible. If you believe that life is hard, you can never catch a break, and you can never trust anybody, your Unconscious will look for examples where that is true. It will even steer your behavior to make it *continue* to be true, perhaps making you avoid sending you that one email that could land you a great new job! Conversely, if your Unconscious is programmed to believe that success is everywhere, guess what?

We will indeed experience success everywhere, and we will see it everywhere as we go about our daily lives.

Think about how *powerful* that is. The world offers infinite examples to justify and support whatever you believe, so it is up to you to decide what to look for. This is a pillar of NLP and other concepts, and we'll get much more into it later.

The most crucial Prime Directive to understand if we are to overcome an addiction is that of *preserving the body*. This means, above all the other decisions we make, self-preservation is key. After all, it's your Unconscious that redirects blood away from your extremities to warm your organs when you're cold, isn't it? No matter how warm your Conscious Mind wants your fingers to be, your Unconscious wins out every time. This prime directive extends thousands or millions of years ago, and exists as an innate part of all life forms. Thus, we usually call it an *instinct*.

This seems contradictory to addictive behavior, though, doesn't it? I've never known a cigarette smoker who, once told they are killing themselves, said, "Really?! Oh my god, I didn't know! I'll stop right now!!" So that leaves the question: if the primary urge of the mind is to preserve the body, why would anybody take drugs?

Well, here's what happens. When we make a decision, like one to smoke cigarettes, we create a decision with our Conscious Mind. Anyone who says they really want to quit an addiction, but just keeps going anyway, is the victim of a conflict between that Conscious decision and the prime directive of the Unconscious Mind. See, one part of them says "Yes, I must quit," and another part of them says "Why should I?"

But why would our Unconscious Mind, which is supposed to preserve our bodies above all else, allow us to smoke? Isn't that harmful? Our Conscious Mind sometimes gets stubborn enough to override the directive, and convince the Unconscious that smoking helps you meet other important needs.

Sounds wrong, doesn't it? Well, perhaps our Conscious Mind places a very high value on avoiding stress, so it will say, "Every time I smoked a cigarette, I got to take a nice, deep breath in, and as I breathed out, I always felt more relaxed." In other words, the Conscious Mind starts to link smoking with relaxation in the moment. Even though there are serious health concerns, these are put off for the future in order for the immediate perceived stress to be avoided.

At first, the Unconscious Mind doesn't want to smoke, but the Conscious Mind is persistent and manipulative. Whether it takes a minute or a decade, the Unconscious eventually gets on board with the addiction! So now you're mostly (or even totally) aligned with smoking, drinking, or whatever it is you're addicted to.

But what happens when you want to quit? Now you have a problem again. Your Conscious Mind wants to stop the behavior, but usually not strongly enough to completely overrule the unconscious, so there is conflict. The Conscious Mind says, "This is stupid. This is bad. This hurts me." Meanwhile, the Unconscious Mind says "But how else are we going to avoid that dangerous stress? And those deep breaths make me feel healthy, too." So you continue the behavior.

PARTS OF THE WHOLE

What this tells me, immediately, is that you've actually created two separate neurological parts of your mind. These aren't only psychological, but physiological as well. There's a separate part of you that has a different immediate desire from the rest of you. As a result, you can actually feel split, like you're not one whole being.

When we create such a part, it eventually begins to develop different intentions, beliefs, and identities. Most of us have experienced this at various times; most of us probably have a few separate parts of our psychological makeup right now, in fact. This is totally normal, until it starts to cause problems.

(Taken to an extreme, this is actually the basis of many cases involving Dissociative Identity Disorder. Of course, the medical field would have us believe that such a psychosis can never be cured, and that you need constant medication in order to dull the effects. That is absolutely not true. Even though I'm not an MD, I'm very familiar with Dissociative Identity Disorder. It's nothing more than extremely segregated parts of the mind! If one part's behavior, belief, or identity is bad enough—can turn into a separate identity in and of itself. Some people even give this identity a name, and they call it a personality. Then, they seek medical or psychological treatment when all they really need to do is integrate that part back into the whole, so it just disappears. I've seen this happen time and time and time again.)

When separate parts do cause problems, NLP has a great way to address it, called *Parts Integration* therapy. This technique identifies the parts of you that want different things, and brings them into agreement so powerfully that the body actually goes through a physiological change as it becomes whole again, the way it was before the conflict arose.

With my clients, I often do a Parts Integration as part of a Breakthrough session. And every time, we find the one part is seeking to meet the same needs as the other is! One part wants to smoke in order to get peace, and the other part wants to quit smoking because it knows by quitting, it can relax, stop worrying, and find peace. Isn't this interesting?

The objective of a Parts Integration is to find that common value, and use that to reconcile two opposing aspects of ourselves. It is often simple and effective, precisely *because* they're already in agreement about the basic need; this is really just a question of how best to meet it.

For most of us, this feeling of having a part with a separate intention is a part-time phenomenon. For example, some people do not drink "alcoholically" all the time, but only in certain situations or at certain times. In social psychology, this phenomenon is called cognitive dissonance, which simply means that there is a conflict between your beliefs and new information or a new behavior. A separation occurs because one part of the human wants to do or believe one thing, while another part wants to do or believe something else.

We create this part because as rational, intelligent human beings, there's no other way to justify certain behaviors. For example, part of my identity is that of a rational human being. Clearly, a rational human being wouldn't smoke! Yet I, like millions of people all over the world, found myself (in my younger years) smoking all the time. We must find a way to convince ourselves—at some level—that it is okay. Often, this sort of cognitive dissonance is the turning point for the creation of a separate part.

But, thankfully, we can often get rid of these parts without even becoming aware of their existence. Often, simply learning about how we think and why we believe in certain things is enough to get congruence on an issue.

WHO'S DRIVING THE BUS?

This brings us to what might be most important part of the book, the part where we stop being victims and start looking seriously at how we affect our lives. As we become aware of what's going on, it's time to take control.

When it comes to problems of the Unconscious Mind, people often feel like they're not in command of their lives. They'll say things like, "Oh, it runs in the family," or "That bastard drove me to drink." Whatever the words use are, the meaning is the same: they're not taking responsibility for their own lives! When we're walking around with our addictions and our obsessive-compulsive behaviors, just doing whatever our Unconscious Mind wants us to do, we're simply refusing to take the wheel. I always ask my clients, "Who's driving the bus?"

I can't state it any simpler than this: *Nothing is your fault, but everything is your responsibility.*

Let's imagine a conversation between two people for a moment. One of them makes a very good point, but the other tries to counter it. Soon, the two people are fighting over what should have been a simple sentence. Whose fault is the fight?

The answer is simple: *both of theirs.* It's the first person's fault for not stating their point in a way that would have made it easy for the second person to accept, and it's the second person's fault for not identifying the intent behind the point the first person made.

In fact, every single moment in every single conversation is the responsibility of both people. After all, each person is either listening or talking 100% of the time, right? While you're talking, you are responsible for your words, and while you're listening, you're responsible for your understanding. This doesn't just apply to conversations, either—as I'm sure you've guessed by now. It applies to every aspect of your life.

This is perhaps the most essential thing to understand: *Everything that you experience now is the sum of all your prior experiences.* That's right; every single thing, down to that time you got rear-ended, was your responsibility. You could have done any number of things to avoid the problem, but you didn't. You could have done any number of things to make the problem worse, as well, but you didn't.

Now, I know this probably sounds very simplistic to many readers, and that's okay. I only ask you to read through this and take it into the common-sense corner of your mind. Just ask yourself: "If I accepted this, would I be more empowered? Would my life be better?" Most people answer with a resounding "Yes!"

As you read on, you'll probably be overtaken with delight. Becoming aware of the way in which our Unconscious works affords us an opportunity to take charge of how we've been acting and feeling. And because we can take charge of it, we have the ability to make a change for the better. We don't have to be the victims. Let's get back behind the wheel, and start driving our own bus.

CHAPTER 4
OUR NEEDS AS HUMANS

It's time to dive into why we, as individuals, do what we do. This will clearly address the real reason people have addictions, go to 12-step meetings, and go back out with their addictions intact. It will answer why any addiction, regardless of whether it involves drugs, exercise, food, charity, alcohol, sex, shopping, sugar, or anything else, is created.

One of my most influential mentors, Tony Robbins, studied this problem so much that he developed his own theory called Human Needs Psychology. Philosophers over the years have picked up on parts of this theory, which actually started with John Stuart Mill's "Pain and Pleasure Principle," Friedrich Nietzsche's "Will to Power," and Viktor Frankl's "Will to Meaning." But Tony Robbins had the realization that all people seek to meet just six Human Needs, and that all actions can be attributed to a desire to fill one or more of these needs.

According to Human Needs Psychology, there are four basic needs of the mind, and two higher needs. Many people get by in life just meeting the first four basic needs, but never feel the real sense of fulfillment and quality of life that can be had when all six are met at high levels. Let me elaborate.

MEETING OUR NEEDS

The ways that we meet our needs are through vehicles (actions & behaviors), identities, beliefs, and emotions.

Every need can be met through certain vehicles. A vehicle could be your job, relationship, car, charity work, hobbies, drinking, or even the AA program. You can even meet certain needs just by identifying yourself as intelligent, funny, strong, a survivor, or the President.

We can also meet needs through our belief systems as described earlier. We can get our need for certainty from "knowing" that all men suck, or all women are vengeful. Obviously, those blanket statements aren't true, but our minds don't know that. I know, some men do suck, but that's not the point!

CERTAINTY AND VARIETY

We all have an innate need for certainty. Seems simple enough, right? Since the dawn of time, our ancestors have struggled to find ways of being sure of what's coming—from hunting to astrology to government, our inner beings will do whatever they can to be certain.

But what if I told you we also have a need for variety *at the same time?* Said differently, we need to know what to expect, but we also have a need for some surprise! We need sameness, and yet we also need change. These aren't just desires, *these are needs.* We will always find a way to meet them both.

Have you ever known someone who was married for years without much excitement, and they started having an affair? Perhaps what they got most from their marriage was certainty, and their new lover gave them all the variety they ever needed.

Why don't people in this situation simply get divorced? Is he or she a bad person with no morals? Without defending the action, because this is a touchy subject, my intention is simply to explain from a psychological standpoint why that action would and does occur. I do believe there are better ways to handle such a conflict.

The main reason people who "cheat" rarely get divorced is because the fear of losing certainty from the marriage is too great. This is not merely a desire, but a real need. Occasionally, a person in this situation will stay with the new person so long that eventually the new relationship gives him or her enough certainty while still providing them sought-after variety. In this case, the person having the affair will likely end the marriage. However, all too often the new relationship quickly becomes just like the old marriage, with too much certainty and no variety. What do you suppose this person would do now? That's right, they will find it time to move on and possibly have another affair. The pattern starts all over again.

Now, a person in this situation may beat themselves up every day for their behavior. It is not necessarily that they are bad people; they just have a major conflict going on in their unconscious. People will violate their morals if it seems necessary to meet their basic human needs.

Of course, you have never done this: ended a boring and certain relationship just to start a new and exciting one full of variety. You have never grown antsy until another person commits to having a relationship with you, and then found the new relationship boring and certain. The problem, of course, is that the element of new and exciting variety is gone. Starting to get the picture? We all experience this paradox somewhere in our lives.

CONNECTION/LOVE AND SIGNIFICANCE

The next two needs are interesting because they are also in direct opposition: the need for connection and/or love, and the need for significance, or to feel special and unique. We need to have and give love, whether it's to humans, animals, intimate partners, God, ourselves, or nature. We will settle for at least a sense of connection if we can't have love, because connection is the foundation for love. Thus, it still meets the need at a basic level. Furthermore, connection comes much more readily, because it can come in either positive or negative forms, while love can only be positive. At the same time that we need to feel connection or love, we also have a need to feel special, like we are the only one like us in the world. So, how can we stay in rapport and maintain that connection our friends, but be special and unique at the same time? This can be a matter of striking a delicate balance.

A few years ago, I wanted to start a business, because it would make me feel accomplished and significant. At the same time, however, it would separate me from my friends, who were content making the minimum wage. This created an internal conflict between the need to feel significant and the need to feel connected. In such a situation, some of us may abandon the idea of starting a business and revel in the feeling of connection with our friends, because we are taken back into the certainty of our existing friendships. Alternatively, we may abandon our current friendships in favor of pursuing the new business in order to feel significant, and get some variety.

Everyone needs to meet all four of these basic needs, but sometimes it seems that the more we go for one, the more we lose the others.

GROWTH AND CONTRIBUTION

The last two human needs are the higher self, or higher conscious, needs. These are the needs for personal growth and the need for selfless contribution. We know instinctively that everything on earth is either growing or dying, and that we are no exception. We know that part of our purpose is to continuously grow as human beings. We were given a gift of consciousness, and we know that we must use it.

Most of us also feel that life is about more than just ourselves; it's about "we." We know instinctively that life is about contributing to others. We also know this because every time we give selflessly, we feel good, or "right" and aligned with life. These two needs are about making us more and making others more. Life is about growing our spirits and contributing to the growth of others' spirits.

These needs of the spirit are not in conflict; rather, they complement each other. When we give our energy (time and/or money) to a charity, we almost always grow as individuals as well as making contributions beyond ourselves.

Unfortunately, most of us don't go out of our way to meet these two higher needs. Instead, we tend to focus on the four basic human needs and try to meet them by taking the path of least resistance.

Watching television, for example, usually provides an extremely passive way to meet our first four basic needs. Sometimes we even get some growth out of it, say by watching the Discovery Channel or something educational. Because television provides the path of least resistance, we get into the rut of sitting down, turning on the box, and turning off our minds.

Television meets our need for certainty. We get to watch the show we like on the same night, same time, with the same characters. We don't know what to expect this new week on that particular show, so we also get variety. Over time, we develop a false sense of connection with the people we see on TV. Also, if we catch a new show or a sports game that someone else missed, we might feel slightly special and get to tell them about it, which would meet our need for significance.

Thus, the first four human needs are all met, albeit at very low levels. On a scale of one to ten, watching television may meet these needs at a level three or four.

I'm sure you're getting the picture. Every single thing we do in life is driven by the six human needs. Remember that our actions are just vehicles that get us to those needs; they are not the needs themselves.

So doesn't it make sense that addictions to alcohol, drugs, or sex—as well as the 12-step programs we use to combat them— are all just vehicles we use to meet our needs? Just like our careers, relationships, schooling, friendships, hobbies, and everything else, don't addictions meet certain needs?

Let's look at alcohol. When we're out drinking at our favorite bar, having a good time, meeting people and so forth, what needs might be involved? On a scale of one to ten, what level of certainty would you get from going to familiar places, seeing the same friends, feeling that same drunk feeling? Perhaps a seven or an eight? How about variety? New people are always there; perhaps you will black out; maybe get into a fight; or go home with someone new? That would probably rank as a level eight, too. What about Connection? Well, we connect with our drinking friends, and even the bartenders. With all those connections, wouldn't that rank as maybe a seven? Would we get a sense of significance from being the life or the party, the angry fighter, the hot seductive woman, or the person who knows all the owners of all the clubs? On a scale of one to ten, could that be a six to an eight?

But how far does addiction go towards meeting the higher needs? Growth? Zero. Contribution? Zero.

Okay, now this part of theory on human needs is important. Whenever three or more of our needs are met at sufficiently high levels, we create an addiction. You suppose alcohol is the only addiction? Remember, we can be addicted to sex, depression, anger, money, fighting, running, working out, biting your nails, computers, eating sugar, or even shopping? Virtually any action will meet certain needs, and when enough are satisfied at high enough levels, you become addicted to that activity.

The great news is there's an easy way to break free from that addiction. You don't need years of therapy, and you don't have to spend the remainder of your life in a 12-step program. You can simply replace the activity with another one that meets more needs and at higher levels. Thus, a new healthy and happy activity will be one of our focuses. When we meet our needs through many different vehicles, we cease to be dependent on just one.

There are a few steps involved in eradicating an old addiction and replacing it with a new more empowering one, but the basic principle is about transitioning to a new way to meet our human needs. This is actually what occurs behind the scenes in the AA program. Remember, the steps and the meetings are just vehicles.

NEEDS IN THE PROGRAM

What needs did I meet in the program? What about Certainty? Even if I wasn't certain about much in life, I was certain about who I was: I was an "alcoholic." I got to go to the same meetings and see many of the same friends, the same time every week. I knew what to expect, and I knew it's time to share whatever's going on with others. From this, I got tons of certainty: level nine or ten.

Variety? Every meeting is just as different as it is the same. Newcomers come in all the time; there is drama if someone goes out, or hooks up with someone new. There is also a sense of excitement about learning new things about myself through the steps, and having "ah-ha moments" when other people share in meetings. On a scale of one to ten, variety probably gets an eight or a nine.

What about love and connection? The environment of the AA program makes love much more possible than when we are "out there." Love automatically meets our needs on a higher level than connection ever could, so this one is easy. The love I felt in the AA program was amazing, easily a level ten, especially compared with the simple connections I got through drinking. At the end of the night, drinking felt empty and completely unconnected and unloved, but the sense of connection I felt with other people in the AA program was real, deep, and lasting.

My need for significance was met in and out of the AA program. In the early days of the program, I felt it on high levels due to my young age. Everyone told me how amazing I was, how great it was that I was in the program given my age, and how awesome it was to get to 30, 60, and 90 days of sobriety. That gave me instant feelings of significance on at least a level eight. And, as the years went on, it continued to grow! After I had some time in the AA program, everyone knew me, I was sponsoring people, and I was taking on duties at meetings. So, my feeling of being special was raised to a level 10 or even a level 11!

Earlier I mentioned that my feelings of growth and contribution were at about a level zero while I was drinking.

How are you really becoming better? To whom are you truly contributing when you drink?

Now, let's look at these needs in the context of the AA program. At meetings everyone shares their stories and, for the most part, gets honest for the first time. We really have no choice but to grow while working on the 12 steps. The same is true with respect to contribution. By sharing our experience, strength, and hope with newcomers, we contribute to their growth and well-being. When we get to the twelfth step, we make a commitment of service for others. When people work the program as suggested, they experience growth and a sense of contribution at levels nine or ten. I'd say my experience was just that: level ten for both.

So let me ask you a pretty basic question. If "being out there" meets four needs at an average level of a five or six, and working the program meets all six needs at levels of nine or ten, which do you suppose most people will gravitate towards? It's a no-brainer: meeting more needs and at a higher level forms a new addiction. Now we are addicted to the program. We need it weekly and sometimes daily. It takes over our life. All of our friends are members of AA. Sounds like any other addiction, only this one is positive... at first.

Remember how even though I continued to grow during my time in the program, my progress slowed down when it threatened my rapport with other members? After about five years in the program, I started to understand that I didn't have all the answers and, more importantly, that the book and the program didn't either!

Eventually, I felt a need to move beyond the people in the program, so I finally broke rapport and moved on with other friends. But whom would I chose to move on with? The group of peers I had when I was using the first time around had very low standards. The next group of peers I found in the program obviously had higher standards, but now I had even surpassed that. So, when I left AA, I had to find a group of peers with standards that were at least even with those in AA, and growing. As we grow, it is a good idea to be constantly raising our peer group.

On top of this, I had to again change how my needs were met. I hadn't done step work for some time, and I didn't have any people I was sponsoring at the time or any commitments of service. Thus, I had stopped meeting the needs for growth and contribution. I still grew as a person, but it wasn't through AA. Because I was getting less from the meetings, I attended them less often, and thus had weakened my feelings of love, connection, and significance. The sense of variety also dwindled as I just stuck to the same group every Tuesday. Even my ability to meet the need for certainty diminished as I began to question my identity as an alcoholic.

So, by that point, all six of my needs were barely being met through the vehicle of AA. It felt very similar to a low point in a love relationship. (Perhaps some of you reading this have either been in a similar situation before, or are at a similar place right now. The next chapter will show you another way to react to times like this.)

Fortunately, there are many, many vehicles in the world to meet our needs. I discovered that once I had my own business, I could achieve very high levels of significance and certainty, as well as tons of variety. When I am a great boss, I feel a great sense of connection or even love from employees and clients. I am constantly growing, as I consider new ideas and ways to serve others. When my work is making a contribution to the greater good, I feel totally fulfilled.

Many people find themselves in this position, but unfortunately their work may become their only vehicle. Imagine a man whose marriage isn't meeting any needs; who has no hobbies, no extra time for charity work, or for enjoying his family. For him, work is everything, because it gives him everything. And he becomes literally addicted to work— "workaholic" is more than just a euphemism!

Now, let's say the business goes under... What is this man left with? He goes through a period of withdrawal, filled with depressive and suicidal thoughts and actions. This is important: most often, suicidal thoughts don't start until we lose our vehicle for meeting our needs and being fulfilled. Now this man needs to find a new way to fulfill his needs, and happens to stop at his nearest bar. Guess what happens next.

This section holds the key to whether we succeed or fail in life. In my view, "succeeding" at life is to passionately enjoy life's journey, and to help others find their way. What I mean by "failing" is to be lost in what the band Styx called "the grand illusion:" the idea that success is having money or having the right person in your life, or that success only extends as far as raising good children. I believe all of those things can and should be a part of a successful journey, but they are not the journey itself. More importantly, they are not the destination.

When we get to the point that our addiction isn't fulfilling enough, we search very quickly for another vehicle and usually find AA, because it seems to be exactly the opposite of the thing that was not working. And, as I described earlier, it begins to satisfy all six of our human needs almost immediately and at very high levels. No wonder it works!

SECONDARY GAIN

When somebody does something, they generally have the innate ability to know whether it's good or bad for them. (I'm not talking about relative morals; that's been the subject of philosophy for thousands of years, and it's not what this book is about.) Everybody has a sort of internal compass that helps direct his or her behavior. That compass asks, "Is this something that's good for me, that I want to do, that I like to do, or that I enjoy doing? Is it a good thing to do, or is it a bad thing? Is it something that I don't believe in, something that I don't want to do, something that's bad for others, bad for me, or bad for the world?"

For example, back when I was using, that compass direction was one of the things that very quickly changed. Early on, my compass pointed North. By North, I mean that using was something I wanted to do. The first few times I used, I thought, "Hey, I know I might get caught, and I don't really want to get caught, but I still want to do this. I do want to get high." Over time, though, the compass started to turn. All of a sudden, it's pointing West, and I couldn't decide what was good for me anymore. Eventually, whether it takes 20 minutes or 20 years, the compass starts pointing South, and you realize inside, unconsciously, that you don't enjoy it anymore.

When I reached that stage, I knew my behavior was bad for me, bad for everybody around me. I could no longer think of anything good about it, but I kept doing it anyway. This is when I realized I had an "addiction."

Secondary gain is defined as "any covert advantage that is not directly related to the professed desired outcome." Tony Robbins once told me that even when people are not aware of the desire to meet human needs, that desire still motivates their behavior. Moreover, it can even create self-destructive behavior. What does this mean?

This is one of the reasons traditional attempts to "break the habit"—even after any physical symptoms have passed—don't always stick. You may go back to the behavior you didn't like, because it meets some human need you may not have known. In other words, what might be a negative behavior at the level of the conscious logical mind, has a positive reward for you at the level of the unconscious mind.

Smoking is an addiction that is commonly associated with secondary gains. Someone says, "I'm addicted to smoking cigarettes. I want to quit, but I just can't." In my studies, I've learned that hypnosis is very powerful at overcoming the problem of Secondary Gains. I've done countless hypnotherapy sessions to help people quit smoking, and everybody who has gone through these sessions with me has, in fact, quit smoking easily and permanently.

People may have every conscious desire to quit. They know it's bad: they know it makes their breath stink, and they know there are 599 different additives, including 46 carcinogens, put into cigarettes. It's clear how bad smoking is for your health. So, people will say, "I want to quit. I don't want this in my body at all." Unfortunately, they have trouble actually freeing themselves from the so-called addiction, because the habit of smoking provides a secondary gain for them. In other words, in some way, smoking meets a basic human need for them.

Let me show you what I mean. Let's take the human need of certainty. Well, by smoking, they are meeting the need for certainty at a level of 10. First, they have an identity: they are a smoker. They know they're a smoker. Second, when something gets crazy or life gets a little hectic, they know they can at least reach for a cigarette. They get to take a deep, diaphragmatic breath, and really "enjoy" that cigarette, taking a break from life.

Another secondary gain associated with smoking is the human need for significance. You may not be extremely unique by smoking, but it may put you in that "upper echelon." When you smoke, and a lot of your friends don't, it makes you significant, precisely because you're the only one in the group "daring enough" to do it. In this case, smoking can meet the need for significance at a very high level.

Let's say you're in school, and the cool kids are smoking, and you are too. Immediately, you have a sense of connection with other cool kids that smoke. Outside the bar, smoking with other smokers builds instant rapport as well.

I just want to impress upon you that there are four basic human needs, and any one of them can create a secondary gain. So, if you know on the surface you're doing something that's negative or bad, but you feel you can't stop doing it, look for a secondary gain. If the change you desire isn't happening, there might be a secondary gain associated with the old behavior. That gain is the reason the change hasn't stuck. As soon as you find the need and address it in a new way, you'll succeed in changing the old behavior.

If smoking is meeting your need for certainty, significance, and connection on a high level, you *will* have difficulty quitting, even after any physical symptoms have passed. So, say you go to a traditional hypnotherapist that may not understand what the six human needs are or who doesn't know specifically how to handle this situation. You may still have difficulty quitting, precisely because you have not addressed the secondary gain problem. When I provide smoking-cessation therapy, The program I use is not any one of those things, because each one of them is a separate and important tool. It's like having a hammer, a screwdriver, a drill, and a saw all in a tool bucket. Each of those things is great, but if you're going to build a house, you might need every item in the toolbox at some point.

When I do a breakthrough session with a client, I do not use only Hypnotherapy, NLP, traditional clinical therapy, or even motivation techniques—we use *everything.* For example, if I am doing a NLP breakthrough session with a teenager, and I discover that they're meeting three human needs on a very high level, we will immediately begin pinpointing alternative ways to meet those needs. Once I can discover the unconscious triggers to their addictive behavior, the other tools make change fast and easy.

(For those of you who want to know more about breakthrough sessions and coaching sessions, just head to my website at www.evolutionseminars.com. You can see about booking one of my trainers or coaches for a private session, or even attend one of my advanced seminars all over the world and learn to do it yourself.)

If you're going to break free from an addiction, it's necessary to find out which human needs you're meeting, how you're meeting them, and find a better, more positive way to meet those needs. You'll quickly forget why you ever engaged in that addictive behavior in the first place!

Some people complain that after they quit smoking, they get fat. But what does weight have to do with cigarettes? Nothing at all. However, overeating may be the way that they've been meeting the secondary gains lost by quitting smoking. Does that make sense? Instead of smoking, they're eating. Someone could just as easily decide to go work out at the gym, couldn't they? The human needs are still being met, but through a much more positive behavior.

Think about it this way. Let's say you have a choice between two different behaviors: one is nasty, bad for you, and hurts you, and the other one is fun and helps you. They both meet the same human needs at the same high levels, which would you choose?

Sometimes identifying the secondary gain involved in an undesirable behavior and seeing a new way to meet it enables a person to drop the behavior immediately, easily and effortlessly.

The only thing that might encourage someone to hang onto it is that identity of an addiction. When we let go of that identity, it becomes a simple question of "What needs am I meeting? How am I meeting them? Is there a better way?" Then, it is just a matter of choosing the more positive behavior. The old behavior becomes a non-issue.

CHAPTER 5
BELIEFS AND IDENTITIES

I grew up in an average home, had average opportunities, and my parents went through average struggles. My Dad had issues; my mom had issues; and my brother, sister, and I had some too.

(I love my family dearly, and am overflowing with respect for all of them, individually and as a family unit. My simple point is that I grew up in the middle—not rich or healthy in any way and not extremely poor with high dysfunction. We really were right in the middle.)

As a typical child, I went through the same developmental stages as the vast majority of people. And that meant that, as a small child, I began to realize (as most children do) that not every need was being met in the way I wanted it to be met. That forced me to start to adopt what we call an *identity*, a way of constantly reminding myself that I have what I don't. Whatever the identity, it's created to help to serve whatever needs we lack.

For instance, if someone grows up amidst uncertainty, because maybe their family was moving constantly, that person may unconsciously decide that having absolute certainty is the most important thing in life. So, as a child, he or she begins to design a life around the identity of a "certain" person.

Parents are only one of many factors that create an identity, but they are an important one—especially when children are very young. A child could develop an identity very much like that of their parents (or very un-like their parents) in order to meet their needs. A child can live an entire life yearning to "be like Dad," simply because they crave the security and certainty that their father seemed to radiate. But these needs aren't the only driver for our identity.

MEANINGS

What really shapes our identity is the meaning we attach to our experiences. Meanings show up everywhere in life, and they are subjective and unique to each of us: when someone says something, it can mean one thing for you and something completely different to the person next to you.

Meanings are created every time we see, hear, feel, taste, or smell something, and are a very important aspect of our memories. In fact, meanings go hand-in-hand with our memories, which are created and stored in three main ways.

First is our Internal Representation – basically, our mind. It's made up of two parts: our sensory memory (often, a visual picture we hold in our minds' eye) and our self-talk (which comes from the language we choose to use in our minds). If I say to myself, "He is mistaken," that would mean something different from "He is wrong," or "He is a liar!" One word can totally change the meaning of a situation or an act. Language is our way of communicating with our own brains to create a meaning out of an experience.

The second filter is usually overlooked, but is just as important: our Physiology, or how we hold our physical body. We'll react to something differently depending on whether we're slouching, jumping up & down, or crashed out on drugs, and that different reaction will create a different meaning for that moment.

Third, and key to the process, is the formation of beliefs; that is, deciding what's true and false. These form throughout life, but the most deeply-rooted beliefs start when we are children, and help to form our identities. When I was a kid, I formed the belief that "It is better to be non-confrontational" in reaction to what I saw as my father's harsh temper. I could have adopted any one of many different possible beliefs, based upon many different possible meanings I could have given to his actions, but I chose this one. To this day, major conflict or confrontation is not in my belief system.

This concept of "beliefs" will show up quite often throughout the book, and are essential to the formation (and destruction) of identities. But why do we need them? And why do they impact so many areas of our life?

BELIEFS

As you'll remember from Human Needs Psychology, one of our basic psychological needs is for certainty. In a world that is ever-changing—where the only constant *is* change—we yearn for sameness, or certainty. If everything on the Earth, our relationships, and even our own body changes every moment, how do we get the certainty we need?

Well, If I believe something is true, that means I'm *certain* it's true.

We all adopt two different types of beliefs in our world: Specific Beliefs and Global Beliefs. Specific beliefs are situation-specific, and have less of an effect on the rest of our lives. They really only apply when we are with a certain person, or in a certain situation. These can be things like: "I'm terrible at math," "I'm a great athlete," or "My dad is just stressed." Notice the key words are a person or a distinct area of life.

Global beliefs are more pervasive, because they do not stop at the specific person or situation. Rather, they will affect how you feel about everyone you come in contact with, in any situation. They also deal with absolutes, such as: "Life is painful," "Men are angry," or "Kids are a real pain." The last one would affect your interactions with every kid you ever come in contact with! Notice the general nature of global beliefs, and how they can deal with a whole area of life or entire groups of people.

Wow, it seems like beliefs are horrible things! Not true! For starters, beliefs get us through some hard times in life. When we change beliefs, we are able to move to the next level in life. As an alcoholic drinker, one might have a global belief that "Life isn't fair." As we sober up and some of life's circumstances change, one of our beliefs could change to "If you work hard, you'll reap rewards." Do you think that this person will have different experiences as a result of changing this belief? Absolutely. That same belief will likely change again and again, as our lives unfold; a higher-level belief might be something like: "Life is abundant, and I deserve unconditional love." Getting more and more useful, right?

Beliefs are really nothing more than a feeling of certainty about what something means. We don't question our beliefs, because we have convinced ourselves that they are true. How do we do that? How do people get so darn certain about their beliefs, and especially about their negative beliefs?

REFERENCES

For any belief, we can always find some sort of evidence from our past or present to support it. These pieces of evidence are what we call References, and they're the reason we believe with such certainty.

See, our brains unconsciously work like a debate competition. There are multiple sides to any uncertain situation, and each team is told to argue opposing sides. Whichever team wins the debate also wins that aspect of our mind, at least for the time being, and we move on to the next uncertainty.

The interesting part is just how many facts and valid arguments can be made for each side. A great debater can create a case for or against any belief, no matter what seems right or moral at the time. To make valid arguments, teams will cite facts, experiences, quotes, and news articles; just about anything. These References form the beliefs of the team, and we do the same thing in the world of our minds. We unconsciously determine the belief we want to have, and then look for references to back it up. We always find them.

There is actually a part of our minds called the Reticular Activating System (RAS). The entire job of the RAS is to scout out and locate things that are relevant to our lives. With all of the information coming into our experience every second, the job of the RAS is to filter out important information. Have you ever bought a new car, and then started to see that car everywhere on the road? How about buying a new article of clothing, then begin to notice people wearing it? Did the car or the clothing just appear? Did everyone spontaneously just go and buy your stuff!? Of course not! They were there the whole time, but were not relevant to your life until now.

When we create a new belief, our RAS goes to work and begins looking for new References to back up that new belief. We say, "Yeah, and come to think of it, my last boyfriend did that too! I guess guys are like that." The RAS automatically makes the connections for you.

As we grow up from being children, these beliefs begin to really take form, and we start to become troublemakers, overachievers, quiet, loud, loving, or shut off.

Is this starting to make good sense? Great.

IDENTITY

As we form these beliefs, we do probably the most important thing we will ever do in life: we create a statement that goes like this: *"I am _____."* When we say "I am" something, that is a statement of belief about ourselves. When we say it often enough, it becomes our identity. Therefore, a belief reaffirmed over time will become an identity.

This concept of identity being created out of our beliefs is crucial, because the reason we fail to change our lives is, at its core, our identities. The strongest will in the human psyche is the need to remain consistent with One's identity.

I remember my first cigarette. I did not enjoy that guy! Coughing and hacking, I couldn't breathe. Nevertheless, I was going to smoke. It was cool, and my friends smoked too. So I had to convince myself of my identity as a smoker. It took me years and years to realize what you're about to learn in seconds: that if you could convince yourself that you were a smoker, you can just as easily convince yourself that you're not!

As you probably know by now, even our bodies are not solid. They are mostly empty space between atoms' electrons. Our electro-physical bodies are in constant flux, as science and quantum physics is now proving. Our cells die off and are replaced with new cells. In fact, every seven years our body goes through a total change! Every cell in your body *didn't exist* seven years ago.

42

When we look in the mirror, we don't see the same face we saw yesterday. However, what we do see resembles that face so closely that we create an identity of how we look and hang on to it. Have you ever looked at a picture of yourself that was taken, say, 10 years ago? Different, isn't it?

Luckily, most of us can change our belief to align with what we look like now, instead of what we looked like 10 years ago. In fact, we unconsciously destroy old beliefs and install new ones constantly, as we find new References strong enough to cause us to change. We can also do this consciously.

UPROOTING BELIEFS

But, my students often ask, why don't we just change all our beliefs so we can be happy? The answer to this is simple: some beliefs are more deeply rooted than others.

Most, if not all, addictions and other problems have an underlying root cause—whatever it was that first led you down the road that ended up in addiction. Whether the underlying problem is a limiting belief system, negative emotions, negative neurological associations, or limiting decisions, finding and changing the root cause is the solution.

The work I do makes a change that's not only immediate, but also permanent. I've had people change things in a single weekend that they had gone to therapy every week for seven years, at a $150 a pop to address. Do the math, and the average therapy bill is about *$7,800 a year.* After 7 years, it would cost $54,600, and usually the problem isn't even gone!

Not only is that expensive, but also it's a lot of your life spent talking about the problem or the issue, looking back at what you don't want to do, and trying to understand it.

That is precisely the reason I stopped going to 12-step meetings. Even though they really work for some people, I found that we constantly were talking about what we couldn't do. Like I've said earlier in this book, some folks in 12-step programs are absolutely beautiful souls. They are wonderful people who get together and talk about what life is like today, the kind of people they've become, what their characters are like, and how they share gratitude with the world. That is awesome.

Unfortunately, that element only represents about five percent of the meetings. The rest of the sharing was the opposite. It was about having the identity of an alcoholic or an addict, or about having a disease, and what would happen if we ever used again.

When we put that much effort or focus into something, the Law of Attraction brings it to us. You'll learn in an upcoming chapter why this works: wherever your focus goes, energy flows.

Our mind is the greatest film editor in the world, because we delete, distort and generalize our experiences. We can take any memories, facts, quotes or experiences we want and string them together, cut out parts, add other parts that were never there, and create a belief from them.

Just like the debate team that needs to cite references in order to win, we search for references to prove our unconscious beliefs to be true. Sometimes, we even make things up! If some piece of evidence or experience doesn't fit with what we believe, we will often just force the fit by attaching a false meaning to an experience or someone else's actions.

I'll give you an example. Perhaps I believe that "My friend John is honest." I have enough references to back it up, so I don't question John's motives. But what happens if John takes a book from my house? I justify his action, because John is honest, and I have to maintain my belief. I would assume he wanted to borrow it and maybe forgot to tell me. To me, that's the only rational explanation. Even if someone else begins to question John's morals, I'd back him up.

I do this because we always fight to keep an existing belief over a changing one, especially if changing the belief would hurt my connection and certainty with John.

However, once enough people ask about John, and maybe give other examples (References) of his dishonesty, I'll finally begin to question my belief. I'll go back through all my old References, and compare them to the new ones, reigniting a debate that might end up with me no longer trusting John.

In order to change a belief that is not serving you well, begin by questioning your references. Did everything that happened *actually* happen that way, or are you assuming too much ? Questions lead to doubt, which leads to changing a belief.

This is actually harder than it looks, and is probably why no one has an absolutely perfect life. Have you ever noticed when you question people's beliefs they run? Since certainty is so important to us, they want to maintain the identities they have built up in the ever-changing world.

I had an intriguing experience on a flight to South Africa. I was standing around in the back of the plane (as you do on a 12-hour flight), talking with a couple other passengers. We were having an interesting conversation, which moved into the idea of beliefs.

The man sat down, and I continued with the woman. I just asked a few questions about motives and beliefs. I said, "Is it possible that two different people could do two very different actions, but have done them for the same reasons, such as to meet the same basic needs?"

"Maybe Hitler was simply meeting his need for significance," I said, referencing another basic human need, "by attempting to create what he called the supreme race and committing massive genocide; while a Fire Fighter in New York City meets his need for significance by rushing into a burning building, knowing he may die." I explained further, "I'm not condoning the behavior itself, and I'm not talking about evil or good, just asking a question of where peoples' motives come from. Is it possible that both people were trying to meet the same needs?"

The woman could not have gotten away from me fast enough! All she heard was "I agree with Hitler," even though I'd said no such thing. I didn't even disagree with any of her beliefs – I only asked a question. But something in the conversation caused her to question a deeply rooted belief, and she ran. It can be a scary thing, changing beliefs and your identity.

This happens fairly often in the realm of religion. Even though many religions exist in the world, people with a lifelong identity connected with a certain faith or sect usually will not allow any doubts or questions to impinge on their identities, to the point of starting a war! Yet others, when presented with enough new References, might realize that another religion makes more sense for them. They change their belief, and become "born again" or "converted."

Now, as we apply this theory to the wonderful world of addiction and recovery, it becomes really interesting. What I am about to say will likely come as a shock and may rock the world of addicts, alcoholics, and counselors. Nevertheless, I must share it, because I know it will save the lives of those who understand.

YOU DO NOT HAVE A DISEASE!

Any of you who don't completely agree with this statement, answer just one question: Is it possible that someone might get upset with this solely because I'm questioning one of their beliefs? Am I questioning a belief that has become so permanently entrenched one might even call it their identity?

This is perhaps the most crucial thing for us to learn. Identities get entrenched, and confronting them becomes painful at times. But that's just an obstacle, one formed simply of words and ideas. Massive growth is just on the other side of that obstacle, so sliding right through it is the easiest way to move forward.

PUTTING THE PAST BEHIND US

There were once twin boys who grew up in the same household with a very abusive father. This man would come home drunk and use drugs in the house. He was never around, and when he did come home, he would beat his wife and both boys regularly. He ended up in prison and was eventually killed. The boys were raised by their mother, who had to go out and get two jobs just to make ends meet.

A writer found out about the horrible childhood of these twin boys and was curious about how they each turned out. Surely, their lives would be some indication of the torment of their past. The writer eventually discovered that the boys had grown up under identical circumstances, but at some point had branched out to lead very un-identical lives.

One boy had begun using drugs early on, started stealing, and ended up going to the same prison in which his father had been incarcerated.

The second twin grew up and went to college. He started a great career, married a beautiful woman, and had children of his own. He is now living a very successful life in all aspects and contributes to community centers for children.

The writer went to interview both of them, one in prison and one at home with his family. Now here's the interesting part. The interviews went okay until the writer asked them an identical question. Surprised by the answer, he concluded the interview with gratitude and went on to write a fabulous article.

I've heard every story of destitution in the rooms of AA. Some of these destitute people had wonderful childhoods and some came from drug-addicted families. But I've also heard many stories about horrible childhoods from people who are now great successes in life; spiritually, emotionally, and financially.

Remember, we usually make beliefs from References in our pasts. But when you identify with the past, you tend to stay there. What's more, "there" isn't even real. It consists of beliefs you've made about the past, and constructed memories.

You know what that means? Our past does not equal our future! We very literally decide our future each day, through our thoughts.

In my sessions, there's no need for me to ever hear someone's back story in order to explain why they do what they do. I know their present is shaped by meanings and beliefs.

The past does not equal the future, *no matter what.*

If beliefs don't depend on our past life and results, where do they come from then? WE MAKE THEM UP! Like I said earlier, we can always find References for any belief we can think of, so we have the ability to change any belief, based upon the future we want.

By the way, the question the reporter asked the twins was this: "How do you see your father's role in shaping your destiny?" Without hesitation, both boys said the exact same thing, "With a father like that, how else could I have turned out?"

FROM THE FUTURE

Imagine this for a moment: the year is 1953. No runner has ever broken the 4-minute mile. Everyone is certain that it's beyond human capacity. Every time they try, they fail, and become more and more convinced that it's impossible. For nine years—an eternity in track & field—the world record time remained

Let me qualify that: everyone believed that, except one man. This man absolutely believed that it could be done, and more importantly, he knew that *he* could do it. Every time he ran slower than 4 minutes, this man used the failures as feedback, knowing that at some point in the future *he* would be the one to do it. The man kept running as fast as he possibly could, collecting feedback, and then running even faster. He had been running for years and years, until one day the judges looked at the stopwatch with disbelief: 3:59.4. He had done the impossible.

This man, Roger Bannister, was named the first ever Sportsman of the Year, had two movies made about him, was knighted by Queen Elizabeth, and a British 50-pence coin was minted commemorating his achievement as the fastest man in the World.

All this, despite the fact that Bannister's record lasted just 46 days (his archrival John Landy broke the record by more than a second). In the next 12 months, at least a dozen other people broke the 4-minute barrier. Now men of all ages, from high school to 40+ years old, are routinely running 4-minute miles. Only after Bannister's success were other people able to change their beliefs about what was possible—and their results changed along with it.

Those who create their beliefs based on the future they want to see get rewarded. Unfortunately, most of us are stuck creating our beliefs from our past experiences. As John Lennon said, "Imagine." Imagine the future of your dreams, and take your beliefs from that!

So what? What does all this talk about beliefs and identities mean for us? I simply invite you to take a look into your own life and at the beliefs you may have created. If you believe you are an addict (or a recovering addict), what's the benefit of that identity? Where was it created, and what was driving it in the first place? Could there be a more empowering belief or identity for you, based on the new future you want to create?

CHAPTER 6
MAKING NEW FRIENDS

RAPPORT

When I found AA as a young man of 17, there were many changes in my life. But looking back, one change stood out above all the rest: my peer group.

Let me elaborate.

Earlier, we talked about Connection as a basic Human Need. To different extents, we all have a need to feel connected to other humans and to ourselves. In order to create this connection, we build rapport unconsciously. Rapport is simply a harmonious relationship based upon similarities. Because of this need, we tend to become like the people we are around.

There have been numerous studies on rapport between children, adults, men, and women. In NLP (Neuro-Linguistic Programming), rapport is a staple. All processes and therapies must be done while in rapport.

A brilliant professor named Giacomo Rizzolatti made a discovery in the 1990s studying monkeys. He found that the monkey brain contains a special class of cells, called mirror neurons. These neurons seemed to engage whenever the monkeys saw an action being done around them. The monkeys' brains acted just as if *they* were doing the activity being witnessed. The brain functioned the same whether the monkeys were doing the activity themselves, or simply watching.

And it doesn't stop at monkeys.

Dr. Rizzolatti believes that the brain cells in *humans* seem to act the same way, since people naturally, unconsciously, take on characteristics of those they are around. Basically, when you witness someone doing anything, even if the activity is as simple as crossing legs, a part of your brain engages in that activity. First you go there in your mind, by firing off the mirror neurons in the brain. But within a short period of time, you'll actually start to physically "mirror" that person—unless they mirror you first.

Next time you're in a room full of people, take a minute to look around. You'll see people unconsciously mirroring each other all around you! Two people may be leaning in or out as they talk, or sitting the same way. And it's not just physical, either: the principle of rapport has an effect on your speaking style, and even your beliefs.

Mirroring can be seen everywhere, but especially with those you consider your peers. A peer is really just someone in proximity to your life whose opinion of you can affect your standards for yourself. A peer can be of any age, background, or current situation, as long as you relate to them in some fundamental way.

Over time, anyone surrounded by a certain group of peers will match the behaviors and beliefs of those peers. Just like water seeks a constant level, people seek their own levels. Any outliers will tend to drift toward the behaviors and beliefs held by greater numbers.

Imagine for a moment a group of friends who are all rather lazy in life, content with drinking beer, watching TV, and hanging out night after night. Now, imagine one person, we'll call him Stan, joins the group. Stan's used to a more active lifestyle, and rarely drinks. But, despite his past, he'll very likely begin to behave like the group, in order to maintain these new human connections.

Sometimes, Stan might try to persuade all the friends to get off their butts and find new things to do. This might work once or twice, but if the center of gravity of the group doesn't change, Stan will find himself fitting in to the group's old habits yet again.

There's a third choice, however, that's often forgotten about: Stan can actually leave the group to find other peers who are more like him. This happens least often, because the loss of connection can be so scary, but it's also the most powerful catalyst for change.

STANDARDS

One peer group is not 'better' than any other, but they all have different levels of standards that play out in life.

Another word for "standard" is a "minimum"—the lowest acceptable option. People's financial standards, for instance, can range from "As long as I get the bills paid," to "As long as I get the bills paid on time," to "As long as I have total abundant wealth, enough to share with my family as well as charity." We have standards in every area of our lives. These are usually only spoken unconsciously, but we all adhere to our many standards for life.

Standards, like beliefs and behaviors, are drastically affected by our peers. But the principle of rapport doesn't only bring people down; luckily, it works the other way around too.

PUTTING IT ALL TOGETHER

If your peers are the single most influential component of your life, and they all drink and use drugs, hang out and do nothing all day, live with their parents, and black out at bars, then those are the standards and behaviors which you'll unconsciously seek to mirror. These people might think recovery is only for the "weak."

If one of those friends gets a huge kick in the pants, maybe in the form of a divorce, a DUI, or a close call with death, they might go into AA despite the beliefs of their peers. There, they'll actually begin to form some new friendships, which turn into new peers, and which may eventually replace the old group.

And these new peers have higher standards. Most of these people work, have fun without drinking, spend time with their families, have homes, and even a little money. These standards on average are much higher than the standards of the old peer group. It's no wonder that when someone really becomes a part of the AA fellowship, his or her life starts to improve.

That's why joining AA was so effective for me: coming to meetings filled with people striving for something new, something better, gave me the opportunity to easily leave my old peer group behind.

You see, at that point, these new people had what I wanted. I was, as most of us are, drawn up towards my new powerful peers in my program family. During this period, we achieve, love, get, give, and start to live with passion. We enter into better loving relationships. We move into a house, and get cars and maybe even a boat. Perhaps we have great careers that were never possible before, and now we're working hard and making good money. Things are definitely much better for us compared with where we were before, and for most anybody's standards.

If my standards could be rated on a scale of one to ten when I was drinking, they likely would have been a two or a three. Not the worst, but there was a lot of room for improvement. Just from being around the rooms of AA, my standards doubled! Now, they were probably a four or five. I had become substantially better than I was, and started achieving great successes in the eyes of my old peers, who were stunned by what I was capable of.

There I was at 17, going to meetings regularly with lots and lots of older people. (Today there are many more young people in meetings, but even back in 1997, there were only a few of us.) The younger people banded together as much as possible, and sometimes we got into some trouble. Just like when we were "out there," we had all the same dramas, fun, angers, and everything else in the program. People got together, cheated, lied, stole, hugged, loved, smiled, ditched work, and got pregnant. Dysfunctional and functional life still happened.

The only difference was that these dramas unfolded more at a level five than at a level two. We had changed some specific behaviors, but we still experienced the same emotions; we never learned how to feel the way we want to feel.

I stayed sober for the next six and a half years, gratefully incorporating the program deeply into my life. I really felt great on a regular basis, but after around year four or five, something had started to shift. These new friends (for five years, by now) have decent lives. Most don't live extraordinarily or do great things. They live ordinarily and do good things. But there was more. My peers in the program were still playing life at a level four or five, but I had started playing at level six.

This was my tipping point.

Once you're past the tipping point, you start realizing how high your standards have become, and staying with your peers becomes more and more difficult. I was confronted with the same dilemma as Stan: for me just to stay at level six, I was trying to bring up 99 percent of my AA peers! That was hard work.

I believe almost every growing and searching person goes through something like this. While we're in it, we don't realize what's happening, but we all seem to start questioning life again at some point, and it seems to revolve around how we compare to those around us. For some of us it happens just a few times, for others it happens regularly.

When faced with this, some just settle in for a few more years, lowering their standards to match those of their peers. Others, in order to "change things up," might try going out with their old peers again, starting to drink or use drugs, and start a cyclical struggle that lasts for quite some time.

What I want to shed light on is the third option: of finding new peers that stimulate and challenge you, who are already what you want to become, and who want you to be better than you are. Surrounded by a circle of friends like this, you have almost no option but to rise to the occasion.

CHAPTER 7
SELF-ACTUALIZATION

For those of you reading who have never been through the 12 steps of AA, I want to make two distinctions: One, that AA isn't necessary to be free from an addiction, and two, there is massive value in the 12 steps themselves.

As I've stated before, I'm not choosing sides on the issue of AA. I'm not advocating it as the only way, but I'm not bashing it either. I believe the 12 steps of AA represent a path that works for many, bringing them to a place where they can live a full life. They can certainly be used as a springboard for deeper spiritual, emotional, or business progress.

I believe that the spiritual principles behind the steps have immense value on their own, without the specific steps. Almost anyone would agree that humility, honesty, love, compassion, and gratitude are principles that can guide all our lives for the greater good, regardless of religious background.

Also, going through the steps gave me my first true look into myself. Like most, I had a hard time with this at first. Soon, I realized this wasn't because I didn't want to look at myself, but because it always seemed as if all that mattered to AA was my past. When I first began attending meetings, all we talked about was where we had been and which parts of our past we wanted. But at 17, most of my past hadn't even happened yet!

Yet the program and the steps have room for improvements and for distinctions to be made. Certainly major changes can and should be made in the teachings and in the practical steps. I won't go through each of the steps in this book, but I will break down the main sections of what we call "Step Work."

STEPS 1-3

The first three steps are certainly useful for most people, because they deal with identity and faith (in God or a Higher Power of some kind).

These steps teach a person to let go of the control we always thought we had, and how to allow something more powerful than ourselves to guide our lives. After Step 3, we're able to trust in some sort of grand design, which gives us a lot more opportunity to progress without fear.

There is a fundamental flaw in these steps, unfortunately: you are supposed to create a new identity that says you are an alcoholic and will be for life. They have you face the "fact" that you have a disease that is incurable. Every day, you affirm that you are broken.

STEPS 4-10

These steps deal with understanding the past, correcting patterns in yourself, and amending past mistakes that you have made with others. These steps are powerful, because of the high level of honesty involved in looking at our past and amending mistakes. But, sadly, the trip into the past does not uncover any real motives for behavior. It is like traditional regression therapy with no clear outcome; just reliving the past pains while running the same neurological pattern.

Steps 11 and 12 are the spiritual journey of prayer, meditation, and sharing a message. These last two steps are the most crucial part of the journey, yet are realized the least. The message we are to carry to still-suffering alcoholics is that there is hope. A good message, if that's where it stops. However, according to AA, any "hope" lies only in taking on an identity of a sick person for whom there is no cure; only "a daily reprieve."

MY (BRIEF) STORY

I found a sponsor who guided me through the first few steps. He was an amazing man, and at the time I looked way up to him and who he was. At that time, I was a juvenile, used to skateboarding around town looking for drugs. Pretty much anyone could be admired, and he was no exception with his beautiful outlook on life and warm smile. I ran into him recently by chance, and I still see him as a good man with a warm heart.

I switched sponsors, however, when I got stuck on my fourth step (as many do). I started over again with a friend who was only a couple of years older than me, and whom I also really looked up to. Yet I went through the same pattern with him as I did with my first sponsor! I worked step four until I felt "stuck," then looked for a new sponsor.

I finally worked the steps with David. He was a bit looser with the program than my previous sponsors had been, and that was just what I needed. He had me start writing what was basically an autobiography. The important parts and the hurtful parts came out, and those got a lot more pen time than the others. This was the purpose of the step for me.

For the first time, I shared the hurts I had experienced from my father, my feelings about school life, and my primitive beliefs about myself. I didn't realize then how many unconscious beliefs I had already formed by age 18 or 19. We went through the rest of the steps, and surprisingly, most came automatically; not really requiring much action or writing. Most of the steps for me were just steps of awakening.

As I got to the twelfth step, I started to get a glimpse of what life was about. I say 'glimpse,' because it revealed only a small part of the gifts I really had to offer, and because it was temporary. I simply began living the principles, rather than trying to understand and write about them. As I lived them, I would run into kids who were new to the program and share the message of recovery.

Once I had gone through the steps, though, I found myself getting stuck in a rut, and began exploring other options outside AA. I looked into different religions, meditations, self-improvement tapes and seminars, psychology, the Power of Nature, the Universe, and pretty much anything that would give me more answers. What I got were a lot more questions, but some very quality answers.

As I studied NLP and other therapeutic modalities, I finally learned the real secrets to being free from my old addictions. These are keys that changed my entire belief system about the program, the steps, alcoholism, addiction, recovery, and pretty much everything else.

For instance, as soon as I started understanding the importance of Identity, I stopped calling myself an alcoholic. Instead, I identified myself as a "grateful member of AA" when I went to meetings. After a few more months, the only reason I stayed in the program and attended meetings was to share with new members and contribute. This wasn't enough for long, and I grew antsy as I began to realize I was no longer in the right environment.

I then started down the road of self-actualization. I believe that road is a journey, not a result, as is all of life. Webster's dictionary defines Self-Actualization as "to develop or achieve one's full potential." Most of us, unfortunately, never get close to living out our true purpose.

There is an ancient credo that says, "Know thy name, and be thy name." To me, "Know thy name" means know your purpose, know your mission, know what you are great at, know your gifts, and know your passions. "Be thy name" means, simply, to fulfill that knowledge! Make your passions and skills your life's work. According to this concept, it would be totally disgraceful if you knew you were the greatest healer, and take great joy in healing others, but then lived a life behind a desk. The communities of ancient Asia were full of a sense of fulfillment, because everyone contributed in the way his or her heart dictated, not by what would make the most money.

I wonder what will happen when we start living that way…

CHAPTER 8
GOTTA GROW!

After six and half years of sobriety, I looked around my AA community and saw a lot of what I didn't want anymore. I watched a lot of people living lives I did not want, working jobs I did not want, making small amounts of money I did not want, behaving in ways I did not agree with, and treating their health how I definitely did not want to treat mine. But, since we become who we surround ourselves with, I was stuck with all those things anyway.

Because our friends, family, sponsors, and sponsees love us so much and want connection so badly, they pull us towards them. Those of us who have surpassed the standards of the group are left with a choice. This juncture is what I call "grow or die," and it happens just as we begin to want more for our own lives than even the best quality people in the program are living. In the program, the choice is simple: there are two options, "working the program" and "going out again." Either we stay on the path, or we fall off the wagon. But I don't believe our options are that limited. There is a plethora of options along the spectrum, not just the two extremes!

People new to AA always hear stories about people that just "went out," and how they should be pitied. I'm probably one of those statistics being shared in the rooms of AA! What AA does not see is that my life is completely amazing today, far beyond anything I ever imagined when I was in the program, and especially before I first got clean.

So as we feel that aching need to grow or die, we come to a choice and make a decision either to move on and grow even more, or to stay in our comfort zone. It is in these moments of decision that our life's journey is really determined. Unfortunately, and yet very powerfully, this same fact holds true for indecision as well.

For me, the choice was clear. If I was going to grow past the perceived limitations of AA, I'd have to let go of my need for connection. Instead of peers who thought I already had it so good and had achieved so much that I should just relax, I wanted peers who would believe that I had made a great start, and who would support me in knowing how much more my life could be. I wanted peers who would be out running, riding bikes, working on big business ideas, working out, serving the community, putting together real estate projects, helping charities, climbing mountains, traveling the world, and be engaged in loving passionate relationships.

I knew that life was about more, and that "more" was meant to play at a tremendous level. "More" was to quit being so damn selfish and think of others beyond my little world. Although I had achieved enough to take care of me and help a few people around me, I thought to myself, "Is your world really so small that you don't want to make a difference in others' lives? You have the leadership and resources within you to reach and help thousands, if not millions!"

I'd hit my threshold (my "bottom," as they say in the program), when you just have to take a leap of faith.

CHAPTER 9
THINK BEFORE YOU SPEAK

Our words have an effect on everything. They are much more powerful than most of us realize. Whole identities are forged from single sentences. "I am a man," I might say. And that's true—to a point.

What about the times when I feel like curling up on the couch to read? What about when I think about puppies and kittens and smile? Men aren't supposed to like those things, are they?

Now it seems like I should add something on to my identity: "I am a man who's not afraid of his feminine side." But then there's certain parts of my feminine side that I definitely try to avoid—soap operas, for instance. What then? "I am a man who's not afraid of his feminine side, except for certain bits and pieces that he feels are *really* best left to the women." You can see how unwieldy this gets, and quick! Imagine what we each do with a lifetime of identities that started innocently enough…

In my experience, there is an alternative. Instead of modifying the identity and creating ever-expanding nonsense, it's much more useful (and easier on the Unconscious) to simply state what *else* I am. "I am a man" becomes "I am a man, and a lover, and an athlete, and a husband, and a father…" I can go on for hours, feeling more and more positive about myself with every word.

TO BE, OR NOT TO BE?

When it comes to creating and destroying identities, there is no more powerful verb than "to be." It's next to impossible to state an identity without "I am" or "I was." This has been taken to the extreme by linguists such as Alfred Korzybski and his students, who have proposed a new language called "E-Prime," for "English, primed of the verb *to be.*" In their view, people would get into much less trouble (and the physiology of our brains would be less effected) if we simply took the entire verb "to be" out of the English language.

What would 12-step meetings be left with? "I ~~am~~ an alcoholic" can't exist. Maybe they'd say something such as "I enjoy alcohol too much," or "I'd like to drink less." Honest, straight to the point, and—most importantly—devoid of negative identity. It took me six and a half years to realize the power of words in my life, and stop identifying myself as broken, but rather as a "grateful member of AA." As soon as I did that, I felt like a changed man. But did those words actually affect me physically?

WORDS & WATER

The movie *What the #$*! do we Know* documents Dr. Masaru Emoto's work with microphotography of water crystals. Dr. Emoto is a Japanese scientist who became very curious about how words and thoughts could affect water. He would put a word on a jar of water and photograph the molecules as they froze. An interesting thing happened: different words had very different effects on the ice crystals. Words like love, peace, and harmony turned the water into beautiful, symmetric crystals, while words like chaos, hate, or anger resulted in crystals that looked malformed, dark, and ugly. This happened every time, and was completely predictable.

There was one line in the movie that resonated deepest with me: "If words can have that kind of effect on water, imagine what words could do to us." After all, our bodies and brains are up to 70% water!

When we refer to ourselves as "alcoholics," "powerless," "broken" or "incurable," we affect our whole beings, right down to each of our cells.

Another interesting breakthrough has been made regarding our neurotransmitters, the chemicals that bridge the gaps between nerve cells in our brains whenever we think certain thoughts or feel certain emotions. In 1986, a discovery by Dr. Deepak Chopra rocked modern science. He discovered that these same chemicals exist in every cell in our body! While most of science thought that neurotransmitters were only in our brains, Dr. Chopra had discovered that our thoughts can literally affect the chemical makeup of our cells.

Clearly, there's a remarkable correlation between belief and health. A patient diagnosed with cancer and told they have six months to live often believes the diagnosis, and lives on for six months, almost to the day. Sometimes, the more stubborn patients choose not to believe the diagnosis—and go into remission and live on. Whatever people tell their bodies, their cells will make come true. Think about that.

A LITTLE MORE GROUNDED

At this point, I know some people are thinking these last few paragraphs were a little too "New Age," full of "love water" and "emotional cells." This next section is for you, and for any who are still having trouble grasping these concepts. Remember, even though the preceding ideas don't have years of science to back them up, science is proving more of what used to be known as "New Age" every day.

So I'll come at the same ideas from another approach. For example, let's look into psychology and therapy. As its name implies, NLP places huge importance on language. As we discussed earlier, every time we say anything, either out loud or in our minds, we're faced with many important realities, not the least of which is the fact that our Unconscious Minds will not make us into liars, so whatever we say again and again, we make true. If we say something like, "I have an incurable disease," even if we don't entirely believe it, our brains and bodies will find a way to agree. Of course, I believe that "in-curable" means "curable from within," which is a much more useful thing to believe. We create actions that will inevitably justify what we have been saying in our heads.

DON'T BE NEGATIVE

Here's another incredibly important aspect to our Unconscious Mind—it *cannot process negatives*. I can't even *write* that without using a negative! Our Unconscious simply skips over words like "don't," "won't," and "not." Basically, this is because our minds think in pictures: every thought is connected to an image.

What happens when I tell you, "Don't think of a blue tree. Don't think of a blue tree, with blue leaves, and blue bark, and blue branches. Whatever you do, don't think of a blue tree."

What did you think of? What picture immediately came to your mind's eye?

Well, your mind created that picture of a blue tree in our mind, right? Even if you're really good, the blue tree comes as a flash before you cancel it out!

That's how the Unconscious works, and that's why you can't "not" do something—as soon as you think of it, that "something" pops into your head instead! In the same way, you can't "not" *feel* something, and you can't "not" *be* something.

So if I said, "I want to 'not' have compulsions; I want to 'not' be addicted." Well, how do you feel "not" addicted? It's impossible to do that. To even begin the thought, you have to form a picture of you being addicted or doing the thing you wish to avoid. What do you think happens when you form those pictures? Right, your Unconscious goes to work proving you right, and leading you right down the wrong path.

If we're ever going to make a change, we need to stop focusing on the things we don't want. Instead, start picturing the behaviors we *do* want, so our Unconscious proves *those* right instead! Instead of depression, let's go for *happiness*. Instead of addiction, let's strive for *total freedom*.

NOMINALIZATIONS

There's another linguistic problem that repeatedly gets in the way of progress; the idea of Nominalizations. Although "nominalization" sounds like a fancy word, the concept is simple: it's a term for a noun that used to be a verb—a "thing" that used to be an "action." For example, have you ever heard someone say, "I can't change that; I already made a decision." They took the process of deciding, and tried to make it into something concrete, something unchangeable.

Let's give this nominalization the wheelbarrow test: Can you put it in a wheelbarrow? I can put a clock in a wheelbarrow, for example, but I can't do that with a "choice." I can put my shoes in a wheelbarrow, but I can't carry around a "decision;" it's not a real thing! Nevertheless, the person has convinced his or her Unconscious that the decision *is* a real thing. That can be a problem when it gets in your way—now the roadblock is big and heavy, rather than a flowing river of possibility.

I have had amazing success with my addiction clients simply by "de-nominalizing" during a breakthrough session. Instead of asking them what their "decision" to smoke or drink was, I take them back to the moment when they were still *deciding*. It is fascinating to see how many different options were actually available then, besides the one they decided on at the time. With the advantage of hindsight, we are able to turn the decision back into what it really is: an action. Then all the other possibilities open up.

There's another obvious problem of nominalizations in the arena of addiction. Just look at that last word! Therapists and 12-step programs talk about the "fact" that someone has an "addiction." Can you put an addiction in a wheelbarrow? Of course not! By using nominalizations, we are pretending the problems is something separate from ourselves. We do that so we can conveniently ignore the fact that we were constantly *choosing* to *act* or *feel* addicted. Smoking or drinking, it's all just actions we wanted to do repeatedly!

My clients often have major breakthroughs just with this single realization. They realize that when they first started the behavior, their "addiction" wasn't quite so solid. Even if they had symptoms of being addicted, they didn't look at those systems as unchangeable; addiction was still a process then.

As soon as we start to identify it as something solid that can't be changed, the addiction has become a nominalization. Does that make sense? Now that we have given a name to it and accepted it as a "real" thing, we convince our Unconscious to believe we can't change it.

Can a building change into something different? Of course not—it's a building. What about your car—could it become a flower? No way! It's a car! Consciously, you may say, "I'm an intelligent person, so I can do this or that to fix my problem." But our Unconscious Mind says, "Oh, that's an Addiction. That means it's permanent, so we have to carry it with us."

But an addiction is not a tangible, "real" thing. As soon as we turn it back into a verb, our options are wide open. Unlike nouns, verbs *can* transform one thing into something else. The act of deciding can transform a bad "decision" into a good one. But, when we use nominalizations like "addiction," we negate that possibility.

It is *incredibly* important to pay attention to the language patterns you use. Think about the things you say in your own life. Are there actions or feelings you have unconsciously made into "real" things by talking about them as such? Whenever you are in doubt, ask, "Can I put this in a wheelbarrow?" If the answer is "no," you are dealing with a nominalization.

Nominalizations occur in all areas of life, and cause problems in many aspects. Here are some other common nominalizations, and ways to think about them instead:

71

NOMINALIZATION	BETTER OPTION
Give me your trust.	Trust me.
There's no hope for me.	I forgot how to hope.
That goes against my beliefs.	I don't currently believe that.
I don't like this feeling.	I don't like it when I feel this way.
I don't know how to love.	I forgot the steps involved in loving.
There is no communication here.	We're not communicating well.
Our relationship sucks.	We have trouble relating lately.
She doesn't give me respect.	She isn't respecting me.

One of the *most* common, and most important, nominalizations is simply "life." Everyone says, from time to time, "My life sucks," or "My life is great." But what *is* your life? It's not a fixed, concrete object! A life is nothing more than the sum of all your experiences and emotions. When we start to refer to "my life" as a thing, it suddenly feels predetermined, rather than a masterpiece-in-progress. If we don't like "our lives," it is certainly possible to change them if we decide to "live" again!

By the way, did you notice that even the word "nominalization" is a nominalization? Can you put one into a wheelbarrow? Absolutely not.

Obviously, language plays a huge role in every aspect of our lives. This is proven by scientists, psychologists, linguists, and thousands of years of direct experience. It always pays to think before you speak, even to yourself.

CHAPTER 10
THE LAW OF ATTRACTION

I must confess, when I was first told about this theory I was a little skeptical. Like everyone else, I enjoy positive thoughts, but never truly believed that they created anything more than good feelings. How could they?

But then I tried it on, like I do any neat idea that comes my way. What was there to lose? And guess what? If there were one idea that has changed my life forever, this one would be it. Your life will never be the same, and that you'll see the world differently, because of this simple concept:

What we think about, we bring about.

Imagine for one second that everything science has told you about how things are created, done, and moved around within the world may not be the whole picture. The laws of physics and science are in constant flux, and new fundamental discoveries are made all the time! After all, before Copernicus, we *knew* that the Earth was the center of the universe.

Even something as obvious the Law of Gravity is full of mysteries—400 years after Newton, no one knows how it works! There are many competing theories held by the highest authorities in physics on what attracts one thing to another. The Law of Attraction is quite similar to gravity, but it deals not with planetary bodies, but rather human bodies; not with space-time, but with the mind.

The fact here is that we are all energetic beings, made up of energy. Each one of our atoms is made of subatomic particles, which are made of quarks, which in turn (according to the most advanced theories of quantum mechanics) are made of vibrating strings of energy. Each of these strings is, mysteriously, everywhere at once, until we look at it. According to physics, the actual act of observation locks these quantum pieces into place, in exactly the form and place we want them to be.

As we accept this fact, it begins to make sense that maybe it's best not to talk about "not being able to drink," "having a disease," or being an "alcoholic." Our Unconscious Minds and Reticular Activating Systems look for ways to prove us right, and observe our world in a way that locks into place those things we don't want.

This works on a more basic level as well. After all, what is the real difference between ice, water, and steam? It's all still H_2O molecules right? The only difference is the speed at which the atoms are vibrating. Thoughts of disease and powerlessness defeat us, and make us vibrate more and more slowly, attracting only those other things that are least active.

In these ways and other ways yet to be observed by science, we attract whatever it is we think about. If we speak of being an alcoholic, we attract our own alcoholism. And remember, even if we think about not drinking, we have to think about the act of drinking first. Without a positive frame of mind, we attract exactly what we don't want! I can't stress this point enough.

WHERE NO HUMAN HAS GONE BEFORE

Some believe that "the final frontier" will not be space, but the mind. Is it possible that what we see isn't all we have to work with? I believe that what we see in our physical world is just the final result—the manifestation—of all the creative force that went before it.

It's like sitting in a pottery room surrounded by clay. You grab a hunk and begin spinning a bowl. You do this because at the time you begin, you really want a bowl; you could achieve perfect happiness, if only you had a bowl! You begin to make this bowl, and it comes out fairly nice. Perhaps the result is not exactly what you intended, or not your ideal bowl, but very close; just like some of our jobs or relationships right? So you think, "This is pretty good. I'll stick it in the kiln and fire it." Now you have a nice glazed ceramic bowl. The next day you consider something else. You say to yourself, "What I really wanted was a cup! Not a bowl! I better get to work doing what I need to do to make a cup."

So you set to work, trying to take your bowl and turn it into a cup. The bowl's already there, after all, so it must be easy to turn it into a cup! You take the bowl and squeeze it into shape, but it breaks into pieces. So you take the pieces and reform them into a cup-like figure and glue them together. But, because the cup needs to be a different size, not all the pieces fit. Now you get frustrated, or guilty or sad or hurt, because all the old pieces don't fit into the new reality of a cup that we are trying to create.

What would make more sense?

Well, first you have to see the big picture. Take a look around the room. You'll quickly discover that you're still surrounded by a whole mountain of clay! Why not just grab a new hunk of clay and begin making a cup? As a matter of fact, we can use the totally abundant clay all around us to make anything new we choose to create.

At this moment, I am sitting in Sydney, Australia with beautiful Darling Harbor to the west and the awe-inspiring downtown to the east, and I'm just basking in the sun. The skyscrapers reach for sunlight as boats move lazily in and out of the harbor. But I realize that the buildings I see before me are not the clay to work with. I wouldn't tear these buildings down and use the rubble to create more buildings. These buildings are already a final result, of what has been created in the past. All I'd have to do to create a new building is locate the source of the raw materials that I need!

When talking about our minds, our raw materials aren't part of the physical world we can see, hear, touch, taste, and smell. It is a different aspect of the pure energy that makes up the Universe, the Earth, and us. It's where music comes from, and where light is created. It's the dance of energy and vibration, at a quantum level.

This is where desires are born. Thoughts, ideas, emotions, and feelings, creating material things out of the immaterial ether. Every second, our thoughts make us see the world differently, and notice new aspects of the abundance around us. Usually, our thoughts lead us through the world, and we are a slave to whatever they create.

What if we could harness the power of these thoughts, and create on purpose? *But what are they? Where do they come from? And how can we use them?*

ON THE SAME WAVELENGTH

Our thoughts have wavelengths, just like sound and light. We can measure these waves of thought with EEG machines, and you can actually see a printout of your electromagnetic thought waves! We've known this for years, but for some reason most people still maintain that thoughts stay in our heads. That is about as likely as the signals of your mobile phone being confined to the walls of your home! Our thoughts go out into the world, just like light waves, but no walls, oceans, or mountains can get in the way of our thoughts.

If you want to listen to the music on a certain radio station, you must tune your radio to exactly that frequency, right? And, if someone else has their radio tuned to the same frequency, you'll both hear the same music, won't you? That is because you are both tuning in to the same radio waves, vibrating on the same frequency.

Has it ever happened to you that, just as you were thinking about someone, he or she called? Or, just as you were feeling down, an inspirational message came to you from a song or a book? That happens because, just like with the radio, your mind was tuned in to a particular "station." We attract into our life what we think about. It's not a theory anymore; it's a common-sense law of the universe.

There are a few caveats to bear in mind with respect to the Law of Attraction:

RULE NUMBER ONE

Our thoughts must be consistent. If I think about being rich once, but then think again and again that it can't happen and I am destined to be broke, the broke thoughts will win out. I must think about being rich consistently, over time. The more thoughts and energy I put out aimed at achieving a particular outcome, the easier it will be for the Universe to respond to my thoughts.

RULE NUMBER TWO

Our thoughts must be intense. They must resonate with intense emotion. If our thought is just a passing idea, it will have very limited ability to manifest in our lives. However, if we put all of our energy into a thought and use visualization to replay a movie of the *desired* outcome in our minds, that thought is much more likely to be picked up in the Universe.

Any woman who ever continuously "attracts" controlling men has mastered the first two rules of the Law of Attraction— just in the wrong direction! Such a woman has probably consistently and intensely stated something, like "I don't want any more controlling men! Please let me find a man who doesn't control me!" This brings us to the third caveat:

RULE NUMBER THREE

Our thoughts must have direction. We must think about what we want, not about what we don't want. The woman in the above example became very proficient in thinking about the kind of man that she didn't want. Just like our unconscious minds, the Universe does not recognize negatives. Some believe that the Universe is our collective unconscious; others believe it is simply God. Whatever your view, this fits perfectly. So, for a woman to attract a different kind of man, she must avoid any thoughts about the controlling men in her past, or about controlling men in her future. Instead, she must first figure out what it is she *does* want, and think purposefully of finding and attracting a gentleman who fits exactly those attributes. With this thought emanating from her consistently and intensely, that type of person will be drawn into her reality.

How does this relate to the problem of addiction? Let's consider what we do if we believe we, or someone we love, has an addiction.

Normally, we either think, "I hate that he is addicted," or "I wish he would quit doing whatever it is he is addicted to." What do those thoughts do? That's right—they actually activate the Law of Attraction to continue the destructive behavior!

A better thought might sound like, "I wish he *would begin to act* in a certain way," or that he would "realize *all that life can be.*" Or you could say, "I wish he or she *would understand* the contribution he or she could make *with a sound mind and body in a healthy state.*" Can you see how these thoughts produce a completely different mental picture? That means they produce a completely different result?

In 12-Step meetings we talk about being addicted and not being addicted, using and not using, drinking and not drinking. Since the Law of Attraction gives us what we think about, and ignores any negatives, we're constantly producing a life of addiction, using, and drinking—and, therefore, a life of constant struggle.

(If you want to get more in depth into the ideas behind the Law of Attraction, I recommend reading the book *Ask and It Is Given* by Jerry and Esther Hicks and watching the movie *The Secret* immediately, for they both explain the reasoning wonderfully.)

Putting this theory into practice will take mere moments. Simply stay aware of your thoughts, and focus only on what you want to have, what you want to happen. You'll soon find those exact things falling into your lap, where you just have to reach out and grab them!

CHAPTER 11
AN ANCIENT BALANCE

The Buddha once asked his student Sona, "When you tune a lute, do you tune the strings so tightly that they may break? Or do you tune them so loosely that they just lay there?"

Sona replied, "No, teacher, you tune them right in the middle."

"In this way," said the Buddha, "you must live a wise life; neither too tight nor too loose, and then you can come to the liberation of the middle path."

Different explanations have been offered as to why we are here on Earth, and what we are meant to do. While some believe our purpose is to make a legacy, some consider it is simply to love one another. Others suppose it is to win the game, accumulating the biggest fortune or power or control, while others believe that our purpose is to "do God's will," whatever that may be. Many of my friends believe that the secret to living is giving, and to grow our souls to a higher consciousness. As for me, I hope that we can agree that the purpose of life is still up for debate!

There are many people who believe in the necessity of absolutes, either doing something all the way or not at all. This idea has been in place for thousands of years; in fact, reading the ancient philosophers gave me my first clue about the ways in which our minds work. What I realized was that whether we were talking about 2 years ago or 2,000, there seemed to be recurring themes: man has shortcomings, and we want to explain why we are here.

Aristotle was the first to put in writing a complete explanation of this idea: he called it "living in the mean." Aristotle believed all people have personality traits and that each positive attribute has two shortcomings: one that is weaker, and one that is stronger. For example, using confidence as the attribute, the weaker shortcoming would be cowardice—not having *enough* confidence to take action or stand for what you believe in—and the stronger shortcoming would be arrogance—having *too much* confidence, and believing you know it all. Aristotle gave many examples of these character flaws, such as:

ATTRIBUTE	WEAKER	STRONGER
Determination	Indecisiveness	Stubbornness
Generosity	Stinginess	Overcompensation

His point was simple: all of us, in our true and natural form, are perfect. Our egos can get in the way, though, and the more we become separate from what is true and natural, the more our character attributes morph into something either too weak or too strong. Either way, it gets ugly.

In the realm of addiction and alcoholism, the attribute in question would be the pursuit of good feelings. However, it wouldn't be so simple. It would play out like this: the stronger shortcoming would be greed, over-indulgence, addiction, more, ego, uncaring, scarcity (never having enough). As we drink in an alcoholic way, the character flaws rise to the surface repeatedly. In the sixth and seventh steps of the 12-step program, we become willing to ask God to remove all of our shortcomings. At this point, the stronger shortcomings associated with addiction begin to drift away, and are replaced with moderate attributes like confidence, gratitude, love, abundance, caring, and peace. Once we've been sober for some time, however, we tend to tip back to the "stronger" side and experience similar character flaws like ego, scarcity, addiction to the program, or overindulgence in other things, like coffee, cigarettes, or sex. Alternatively, we may swing to the weak side, and just settle, feel unworthy, give up, get lazy, or lose self-esteem.

It's a balancing act. Imagine someone is sitting on one side of a seesaw. They are miserable, stuck there on the ground. Then they let God get on the other side of the seesaw, and surrender themselves to that. Naturally, they start to swing upwards, toward a level, balanced life.

But a strange thing happens as soon as they're close to center. At the first feeling of balance, 95% people either stop growing and start swinging back down toward addiction, or they actually accelerate and swing so high that they're uncomfortable again, powerless to control their progress.

What happened? In the first case, the person forgot about God, who leaves the seesaw, dropping the person back down to earth with a thud. A coward who gains too much confidence too quickly gets cocky, and is slain by a dragon.

In the second case, maybe the person relied *too much* on God, and threw off the balance in that way. This commits them to a life outside their control, where they lack any sort of self-confidence to take the reins of their existence.

The third way, the way discovered by only 5%, is to find a perfect balance. Halfway between confidence and helplessness, between strength and passivity, lies the mean.

Most friends of mine from all ages and backgrounds spent their whole time in the program just swinging up and down on the teeter-totter of life. If they had just slowed down and took the time to find their balance, they wouldn't be stuck bouncing from one extreme to the other.

How many of you can see someone you know doing this right now? Maybe someone you know really, really well? In fact, maybe someone you know so well they stare back at you from the mirror every day? Let's take Aristotle's knowledge and apply it today!

Another philosopher comes to mind: John Stuart Mills. Mills was bred to be a philosopher and to be the best. His father and his mentor taught him at a very young age what he needed to know to advance the theories of utilitarianism. He had an idea called the pain/pleasure principle.

Basically, this principle says that human beings do everything for one of two reasons: to avoid pain or to gain pleasure. People often turn to an addiction for either of these reasons. And, as long as their conscious or unconscious pleasure is greater than any pain, they'll be willing to stay in this addicted state. When the pain exceeds the pleasure, though, the addiction can cease when they choose. This is what we therapists call "leverage," and is key for making any change.

CHAPTER 12
THE REAL SECRET

Have you ever had one of those days, when everything seems to go wrong? Perhaps it starts with a bad night's rest, or waking up late. Then it seems like everyone you meet has a bad attitude. Someone you love is bickering with you; the breakfast waitress is harsh with you; the cab driver won't shut up; and everyone at work seems harsh and disrespectful. You can't catch a break, right? How sad for you, life dealt you a bad day.

Is this true or false? Of course it's false! Life is made up of meanings, not objective experiences, isn't it? As we remember our learning from the Law of Attraction, we are reminded that we attract everyone and everything we experience. If you're surrounded by rudeness and harsh attitudes, how are you attracting it?

In my seminars and sessions, I try to stick to science and truths—simple, quantifiable things with easy-to-follow rules. But even so, I find myself repeatedly sharing my favorite quote from Mahatma Gandhi:

"Be the change you wish to see in the world."

"Being the Change" means not waiting until the world changes. We must start the change ourselves! If you see too much harshness, act with kindness. If you see too much hate, act out of love. If you see too much fear, act out of faith. If you see too much despair, act out of hopefulness. If you see too much sorrow, act joyously. The world around you will soon follow!

Don Miguel Ruiz, author of *The Four Agreements*, says that we are all mirrors of each other. When someone is a beautiful soul and astounds me with their kindness, I know that they are just a mirror of me. When someone treats me harshly, I know that they are also a mirror of me, on some level, maybe even unconsciously.

Do you see, hear, and feel what this really means? If your world sucks, *it's your responsibility.* You are the change! You are the boss!

If everyone lived by this truth, imagine how beautiful the world will be. Indeed, I already see this as I live, by being the change. I can see, hear, and feel it right now.

The best working definition of the word "strangers" that I have ever heard came from an Irish pub, of all places. On the wall, there was a sign that read, "No strangers here, just friends we haven't had a chance to meet yet." So when I write about strangers, now you know what I mean.

I'm sitting on an airplane as I am writing this. My day started in a rush at 5:45 a.m., when I awoke 45 minutes late for this flight. Instead of reacting to the past (in this case, the very recent past of 3 seconds ago, when I overslept), I started the day by asking myself a few questions. First, I asked myself, "Is it definitely true that I will miss my flight?" I realized that the future hadn't been decided, so I got up and dressed quickly. Then I asked myself, "Is it true that I'm going to have a bad day?" I didn't know that yet either—sometimes these days end up miserable, but other times they end up great!

Needless to say, I'd rather have the latter result, so I made a sincere effort to brighten the day of everyone I ran into, including everyone at the airport. They were all strangers to me, and some of them were even treating others in front of me a little harshly. Early morning at a busy airport isn't the least stressful place to be, after all! But my purposeful cheerfulness transformed every interaction I had this morning. When the world needed more love, I behaved in a loving manner. When the world needed more humor and playfulness, I was playful.

Acting like that with the people around me totally broke their patterns of rudeness or boredom. My new friends were smiling, laughing, and hopefully thinking how beautiful the world can be. And guess what? My day's amazing so far.

Even the simple act of focusing on my new (and potential) friends changed my day. When you focus on how someone else is feeling and how you can help him or her feel better, you cannot be focused on yourself.

In order to feel depressed, one must focus only on oneself. They must ponder how bad their life is, how others are treating them, what has happened in their life—see a trend? All the drugs in the world can't shift depression if you focus only on yourself.[1]

For all these reasons, the way you treat strangers is one of the most important secrets to happiness.

---

[1] This statement is not intended to diagnose, cure, or heal any psychological or physiological condition. You are advised to seek professional medical attention if you feel, or have been diagnosed with, depression. This is also not a recommendation to cease prescribed medicine for such conditions. Please see a doctor before making any choices about prescribed medicine.

PART 2

HOW DOES IT WORK?

CHAPTER 13
THE TEN TRUTHS

I know what you're thinking. You are probably thinking it's time for the new and improved Matt Brauning's step-by-step guide: "How to be cured of addiction without willpower." Well, this chapter will not disclose that information, because that information doesn't exist! Everyone's different, and needs different bits of advice.

But there *are* several fundamental truths and concepts that can help anyone live a full life:

1 The opposite of addiction is not sobriety; that's just the flip-side of the same coin. The true opposite to any compulsive behavior is *total freedom*.

2 Our Unconscious Minds are programmed to do and be whatever we tell them to. That means we're in charge of our bodies, from hormones to beliefs, behaviors, and actions.

3 Everything we do, we do for one of six reasons. Any human will violate his or her values and morals to meet basic human needs if they see no other way to do so.

4 Our "identities" come from our beliefs, which were created from our References from the past. They were created unconsciously, and are not necessarily true.

5 We often change our true selves in order to stay within the expectations of our peers. Sometimes we must be willing to change those peers, and elevate the base from which we grow.

6 The language we use doesn't just *describe* our reality: *It creates it.* Be aware of what you say, especially concerning yourself.

7 The key to change is not to "hit bottom," but getting enough "leverage;" that is, associating enough pain with a bad behavior, and enough pleasure with a good replacement.

8 Live life in the mean; extremes don't work for long! When you have been living by one extreme, it is sometimes necessary to live by the other for a time in order to settle in the mean.

9 Guilt of backsliding is the number one reason people relapse into old ways. Rather than feel guilty if you "had one", get excited that you have been doing so well! Just keep moving forward.

10 The Unconscious Mind is where all sparks for addictive behaviors occur. NLP and Hypnosis bypass the conscious mind, and can solve the root cause of negative addictions.

By now, you know that addictions aren't what we were taught they were. And, since you're still reading this, since you've come all this way with me, you know that it's time to decide to change now.

TOTAL FREEDOM FROM ADDICTIONS

CHAPTER 14
BARCODES OF THE BRAIN

Now that you understand the basics of your unconscious mind, it's time for some situation-specific strategies for addiction intervention. If you've read everything until now, what's coming up will just make sense.

How would you like to figure out how your brain stores your emotions and feelings for everything you have ever encountered? How do you know how to feel about your favorite foods? Or about the sunset? Or your home? Or even your mother?

Well, it's simpler than you might think. See, our unconscious minds use a type of barcode system when interacting with the world. These barcodes tell us unconsciously how we should feel about something specific, like food, or time, or people, or things. For instance, you have a barcode for chocolate, which perhaps tells your mouth to drool with anticipation. And you have a different barcode for oysters, which perhaps tells your stomach to turn. What's the difference?

It's just that each one has a slightly different barcode. And guess what?

We can change the barcodes.

A lady from a weekend event was completely addicted to Coca-Cola. She was 70 years old and had been drinking at least multiple cokes a day since she was 5 years old. And she was paying the price, by being overweight, unhealthy, and high risk for diabetes.

I started working with her brain's coding system. 10 minutes later, we put an ice-cold bottle of Coke in front of her... but she didn't want it. In fact, it made her stomach turn!

I saw her 2 years later at a health conference I was speaking for. "Matt, Matt, I gotta tell you, it's been 2 years, I STILL haven't had one single Coke!

Thank you!"

LEAD INTO GOLD

Imagine taking the barcode from this book and changing one little line. Maybe you make it just a tiny bit bigger. What would happen when the clerk scans the item?

Instead of a book, now it's a *toaster!*

What if you could discover the barcodes for any addictive habit or substance? What would happen if you could easily change one of the "lines" of your barcode for that thing?

Well, in just 10 seconds, you wouldn't feel the same about it anymore. I use this technique in our live seminars all the time to show people how fast and easy it is to let go of food addictions *(See Sidebar).*

SUBMODALITIES

Of course, the barcodes of our minds aren't just black lines on a white background. They're a little more complicated than that, and deal with how we store our memories.

Every time we recall a memory, that memory comes with a certain Internal Representation, which dictates how we think and feel about that memory. Each memory has its own Internal

Representation, and they come to us in five ways, called "Modalities":

Visual (seeing)
Auditory (hearing)
Kinesthetic (feeling)
Olfactory (smelling)
Gustatory (tasting)

The important part of these Internal Representations isn't just whether we see, hear, feel, smell or taste is. The important information is actually a little more specific than that, stored in what we call *submodalities.* Submodalities are, naturally, the subordinate qualities of each of these. Most of us are visual people (meaning we memorize visually), so the visual submodalities usually play the biggest part for us.

When we think about something, our brains usually make a picture in our mind's eye to represent it. That picture in our mind's eye might be tiny, or maybe medium-sized, or even take up our entire field of view. It might be near us, or far away; bright, or dim. It could be in color, or black and white. Maybe it's running in your mind like a movie, or it might be a still picture. Then, there's the location: where is it on the screen of your mind? Is it on the left or the right? Is it on the top, bottom, or right in the center?

Sometimes we actually hear something in our mind. What then? Well, if two people say the exact same words to you, but in two different tones, you may get a very different feeling each time. That's tonality. The tempo, or speed, of the words or sound in your mind is important as well. You never know which submodality will have a profound effect on how we feel!

With kinesthetic memories, we are generally dealing with an internal feeling. Maybe when you think of oysters, there's a feeling that's important. The feeling could be hard or soft, it could be rough, or smooth. Is there a lot of pressure, or not much? Is there movement to the feeling, or is it stationary? What is the location? Is it near the throat, or in the chest, stomach, or lower?

Here's the great part. You see, *every problem is a problem of our imagination, and every solution is a solution of our imagination.* So the problem of being addicted to a particular substance, food, or even behavior is simply a problem in our internal representations. Even our beliefs are encoded with submodalities.

For example, what if I asked someone, "How do you feel about love?" Maybe they get a picture that's kind of shaky, dim, and black and white. But maybe when I ask that same person about loneliness, their picture is solid, bright, and full-color. Do you think the person is more certain of love or loneliness? Which one do you think they're going to attract into their life?

I used this technique with a student in an advanced course. I asked her if there was a belief that she didn't really believe was true, but which would be useful if she did. She said, "Well, yeah, I'd like to believe that I could finish school and be very successful, but I really don't feel like it's very possible right now."

The next question I asked her was, "When you think of that belief, do you get a picture in your mind'?"

"Yes I do."

"Okay, great."

Now, I didn't ask her to make a picture, because she's not creating this now. This is a picture she has already had for quite some time, stored at the unconscious level. Basically, as soon as she made the decision to adopt this belief, she created a picture. That picture has certain qualities. So I started listening.

I asked, "Okay, where is that picture? In your mind's eye, is it off to the left, to the right, top or bottom, or dead center? Where is this picture?"

She told me the location, and I asked, "How big is that picture? Is it in focus, or is it sort of fuzzy? Is it in black and white, or is it in color?

"Is it near or far from you? Is it three inches from you, three feet, or three yards?

I continued until I discovered all of the visual qualities, or submodalities, and continued on to the auditory qualities: "When you think of this picture, do you get a certain sound?"

She told me she heard her internal dialogue, saying "It's just too hard!" I asked her for the tonality of the voice, and the tempo.

Then I asked, "Was there a certain feeling that was important to you? Do you get a feeling in your body anywhere?"

She said that she got a certain feeling in her gut, so I found those submodalities as well.

KNOW YOUR UNCONSCIOUS

Now, the cool thing about submodalities is that they're unconscious. Nobody consciously sat there and said, "You know, now that I'm beginning to have this new negative belief about myself, I think I'll make the picture this far away, it'll be this size, and it'll feel like this."

This is cool because you have no conscious connection to your submodalities. Therefore, if you ever had strong feelings about a particular food, either negative or positive, it's easy to change the barcode, and your feelings change along with it!

If you said "Chocolate chip cookie" around one of my good friends, he'd go into a drooling fit! I'd laugh, but he'd always say, "It's not funny, it's an addiction. Some people have heroin, I have cookies."

I didn't think it was really that bad until (true story) he woke up in a motel room on the floor with an empty package of cookies next to him, a mostly finished jug of milk held by two fingers, and cookie crumbs all over his shirt. Poor guy, it was time for an intervention!

What if there was a food like that you are addicted to? Would you like to let go of the addiction easily and effortlessly?

MAPPING ACROSS

Now we come to our first true NLP technique, called Mapping Across. It's the one I briefly explained a bit earlier, with beliefs. Now I'll elaborate.

Mapping Across is a particularly great technique to use to change a habit. As we know, addictions can be associated with many things. Obviously, it shows up for drugs or alcohol. It shows up for sex, food, shopping, money, work, and many other things as well. Basically, an addiction comes down to feeling compulsive about something: instead of stopping to think about it, you just do it.

Now, it's important for your well-being that you don't ruin what's great, right? We never want to reduce your choices—instead, we want to *add* to them. See, that arch-nemesis is never really a choice. It's almost an *obligation*—if it's around, you feel you *must* eat it. So, if you could feel differently about that food, you'll suddenly regain your sense of choice, and be able to *choose* when and where you eat it.

Ready? Great!

STEP 1: Decide on one food or drink that you're a slave to, that you just can't resist. Think about it, and focus on the picture that comes up in your mind. For this exercise, we'll call this the Problem Picture. Focus on the Problem Picture, and identify the submodalities (size, location, brightness, color, and motion are usually the most important).

STEP 2: Decide on a food (or drink, if the Problem item was a beverage) that absolutely makes your stomach turn. This should be as similar to the Problem food as possible, but make sure it's absolutely revolting. Think about this item, and focus on the picture that comes up in your mind. We'll call this one the Repulsive Picture. Pinpoint the submodalities of the Repulsive Picture, and compare them with those of the Problem Picture.

Now, you may notice that some of the submodalities of the two pictures are very similar. That's normal—after all, they're both foods (or drinks). Take special care to identify the *differences*—we call these *drivers,* because they drive the change home.

STEP 3: Bring back the Problem Picture, and start to change its submodalities to match those of the Repulsive Picture! Literally use your mind to move the picture closer or farther, up or down, left or right. It might seem simple, and that's because it is! Make it bigger or smaller, brighter or dimmer—whatever it takes to make the Problem Picture line up exactly with the Repulsive Picture.

STEP 4: We're already on the last step: locking it in. You don't want it slipping back, do you? You can always change it back consciously if you really need to, but we don't want to let it change itself unconsciously. So tell yourself something like, "Okay, now go ahead and lock that picture in right there, like a Master Lock clicking into place."

And now, think about that Problem food or drink. Feels different, doesn't it? Can you see and feel how much it's like the Repulsive food or drink now? See, now that they have the same barcode, you're going to react the same to both foods!

Let's go back to that girl with the shaky belief about success. This is a common problem, so you need to know how it ends up!

Now that I'd collected all the submodalities of her beliefs about success, It was time to play with them. I asked her to think of an absolute belief, something she absolutely knew was true. For example, one might say, "I know the sun comes up every day." For her, it was, "I live in Las Vegas." She was certain of that.

I went through and discovered the submodalities of this absolute belief. Lo and behold, that picture had a different location, a different size, and completely different submodalities from her belief about success. Just like with foods, each belief has a different barcode.

And, just like with foods, if we take the barcode from her shaky belief and changed it into the one on her absolute belief, she'll feel the same way about both. She'll feel solid and certain that she can succeed! No therapy, no talking on the couch, no poor me story, no meetings, the belief just changes. Instantaneously.

So I said, "Great, get that picture of the shaky belief that you can't finish school. It's over here, isn't it?" I put my hand out to the correct location.

"Yes."

"Now, what would happen if the picture of that belief was moved over here," I said as I moved my hand to the location of her absolute belief.

"Now make that picture about the same size as the other one, make it that big."

"How do you feel about finishing school?

She looked at me, and said, "It's easy enough."

I didn't say anything. Moments later, she started laughing hysterically, because she got it. In 30 seconds, we had just changed her future. She'd gone from probably dropping out of school to a life of success, all with a simple shift of submodalities.

Now that we've learned one NLP technique from scratch, the floodgates are open, and things just get easier!

SWISH PATTERN

While Mapping Across works well for beliefs or emotional attachments, it doesn't do well for behaviors. If you find yourself consistently and compulsively doing a minor behavior like biting your nails, picking at your skin, or tapping your foot, you need the next technique, called the "Swish Pattern."

What I mean by a "minor" behavior is that there shouldn't be a major emotional reaction when doing it, or thinking about doing it. If we are talking about serious drug abuse, this would not be the total solution, but it could play a powerful role in avoiding the behaviors that lead to the drug abuse in the first place! I use it in almost every Breakthrough session that I perform.

(I want to add a word of caution here, because in the absence of professional help, use of the Swish Pattern should be limited to habits that are really harmless. If your behavior is harming you, harming others, is age-inappropriate, or is extreme in any other way, then there are probably secondary gains and additional beliefs and things that need to be discovered and uprooted by a certified professional. Also, before using this technique, make sure you are in a powerful, resourceful state of mind. If you're not, then you should seek help from a certified professional.)

Minor behaviors like these are, generally, totally unconscious. The person doing the behavior is not generally consciously aware that it even started until it's too late, and they're already in the middle of it! That's exactly why common methods—like putting nasty-tasting stuff on your nails, tying your hands to the bed while sleeping, or even worse—don't help in the long run. Trying to interrupt an unconscious program that has already begun running is like trying to stop a freight train barreling down the tracks! Instead, we need to derail the program before it even begins.

If we're going to do this, we need to discover the trigger—the state or action that cues the problem behavior in the first place. Once we find the trigger, we use the Swish Pattern to make sure the problem behavior is never started in the first place. It becomes inaccessible, and it is replaced by a more resourceful state or behavior.

Finding the trigger is simpler than you might think. Think of a time when you did the problem behavior, and ask yourself, "When did I know I was *about* to do my problem behavior?" Maybe, if you're a skin-picker, you know you're about to pick as soon as you see a pimple in the mirror. Or, if you're a nail-biter, maybe you feel a certain texture on your finger that lets you know it's time to bite.

Just like Mapping Across, the Swish Pattern uses Internal Representations. But it doesn't get into as many specifics of the modalities as much as Mapping Across—instead, a Swish Pattern is all about visual pictures and lots of speed and repetition.

Ready? Let's go.

STEP 1: Think of the trigger for your problem behavior. What's the picture that you get in your mind? Focus on that picture, and then make sure that you are associated: looking through your own eyes, really seeing it firsthand. Then break your state: open your eyes and just focus on something else for a few seconds.

STEP 2: Next, think of whatever would be the opposite of your problem behavior. What's a healthy alternative? What would that look like? This new behavior should be positive (remember, you can't do a "not" behavior). Once you have the positive behavior, focus on the picture you get in your mind.

STEP 3: Now we get to adjust your picture of the positive behavior, to make it *even more desirable!* Focus on the picture, make sure you're looking through your own eyes, and start playing with the submodalities, like you are adjusting a TV. Make it brighter, or a less bright, whatever makes it *feel even better* for you. Then play with the focus—make it sharper, or softer, whatever feels best for you. Play with the color, the contrast, and whatever else makes this new behavior seem like the best thing you could ever do!

STEP 4: Now it's time to set up the technique in our mind. Bring up the picture of the Problem Behavior, make it big, and put it right in front of you in your mind's eye (make sure you're still looking through your own eyes). Then bring up the new, maximized picture of the Positive Behavior, but make it low and dark in the corner. For this picture, make sure that you can see yourself in the picture, like you're watching yourself on TV.

So now, you have the old Problem Behavior as a big, bright picture in the middle of your mind's screen, and you have the new Positive Behavior as a small, dark picture down in the corner.

STEP 5: In one motion, let the new picture leap up and take over the whole scene, with your perfect submodalities, while the old picture shrinks and disappears. They're literally going to switch places, and they'll do it as fast as you can say, "Swish!" Then open your eyes.

Now the new picture should be alone on your mind's screen, huge and right in front of you, with the submodalities that make it *just feel great.* You're not done quite yet, though.

STEP 6: Close your eyes, bring up the old picture big & bright in the center, bring up the new picture small & dark in the corner, then Swish them again! Open your eyes once more. Keep repeating, anywhere from 5 to 15 times, getting faster and faster! *Make sure you open your eyes between each swish, to reset your state.*

Soon, you won't even be able to access the Problem Behavior picture anymore! You'll know when you're done, because even when you try to think about the Problem Behavior, you'll automatically go to the Positive Behavior instead!

The Swish pattern is very powerful. Like I said, please don't use it on a habit that's massively destructive; it is only for a habit that's annoying. If you want to break a habit that may be destructive, or you have any questions about it, contact our office through our website (www.evolutionseminars.com) to find a coach or practitioner who can do a Personal Breakthrough session for you.

PERCEPTUAL POSITIONS

Imagine a relationship that used to be great but isn't doing so well. Maybe it's a pair of friends who fell apart, or a marriage on the rocks. Maybe one person is going through a bout with alcohol or drugs, and the other one just doesn't understand. The two of them start to get into fights. Natural, right? But have you ever found yourself fighting just for the sake of fighting? Maybe the conflict started about a specific issue, like drinking or drug use, but now, all of a sudden, you're just fighting for the sake of fighting. This is when some of the greatest hurts in relationships occur.

How many people, after doing something someone else doesn't like, have ever heard, "Try and see it from my point of view." It's easy to pretend, and think to ourselves something like, "I guess if it were me, then I would feel betrayed." But that just adds guilt or shame onto our already-long list of emotions, rather than fixing the root problem. It's like we're still in our point of view, craning our neck around to see theirs.

Luckily, there's a simple, easy way to actually shift how you see things. It's called a shift of Perceptual Positions. It's similar to, but far more effective than, just "stepping into the other person's shoes." With this technique, you not only get to see a new perspective, but you actually get to feel different as well!

Just like with foods, beliefs, and behaviors, changing the barcode for an argument will completely change the feeling. It's all in your perspective—some perspectives allow for a more rational reaction than others. When you learn how to consciously change your perspective, you'll learn how to consciously master your emotions!

Basically, there are two different ways to see things: "Associated" or "Dissociated." We hit on these briefly in the Swish Pattern, and it matters even more now.

When you're Associated, you're seeing things through your own eyes. We all live our lives Associated, since we see our present moments through our own eyes. When you're in an argument with somebody, you see the other person from your vantage point, correct? Memories and Internal Representations can be Associated if the pictures or movies in your mind appear as though you're looking through your own eyes, seeing what you saw.

On the other hand, when you Dissociate, you're actually seeing the scene or picture from outside of your body. It's as though you're watching yourself on TV. Some of your memories and Internal Representations are probably Dissociated.

There are only a couple steps to Perceptual Positioning, which makes it all the more powerful in its simplicity. What's beautiful about this is that it's what I call "content-free;" it doesn't matter what the argument is about. You don't need to go through what the words are, or who said what—none of that matters. The only thing that's important with perceptual positions, like the other two techniques, is the structure of how we store the emotions. Destroy the structure, and the backstory goes with it!

STEP 1: The first thing to do is close your eyes, but stay Associated into the scenario. You should be seeing the event though your own vantage point. Just take in the whole picture, with all the feelings, and truly experience what's going on.

Let's say somebody's yelling at you because you're drinking too much. One of the reasons you might fly off the handle at them, and then go out and do the very thing they don't want you to do, is the emotion you're having in that argument.

STEP 2: The next thing you do, naturally, is Dissociate. Float up out of your body, and right down into the other person's head. See what *they're* seeing, hear what *they're* hearing, and feel what *they're* feeling. Now that you're there, take in the whole scenario again. Notice how, as soon as you dissociate, some of the emotional charge falls away. Don't worry about the content; simply notice how different it feels, and how the qualities of the picture have changed, simply because the vantage point is different.

STEP 3: Now it gets interesting. Dissociate yet again, rising up out of the other person's body, and right into the vantage point of a fly on the wall! Now you can see two strange people, having an argument. Notice the feelings and energy of the room, and how the overall emotion is different from what either you or the other person was feeling. The qualities of the picture are different, and the conversation's becoming kind of funny! Since a fly doesn't cling to beliefs, doesn't notice who grew up with what belief and whether the other person has a valid argument, you simply notice two people in conflict who just want to be loved and be happy. The fly has an interesting vantage point, doesn't he?

STEP 4: Open your eyes and notice all the ways the situation has changed! Notice how different you feel about whatever you used to be arguing about, and how different the other person's point feels.

I know you wanted it to be harder, but that's all there is to it! It's a fun exercise to do. Try it out, with a memory or with a current scenario. The exercise is perfectly safe; you can feel free to go through it as many times as you want! Enjoy!

Now the next step is to avoid the argument in the first place—to be able to be in control of all your emotions, all the time! Seems impossible, doesn't it?

Well, I have news for you: it's easy.

CHAPTER 15

ANCHORING

To some extent, we're all a slave to our environment. Maybe it's a person who knows how to "push your buttons," or a certain situation just makes you mad every time it comes up. How great would it be if you could be in total control of your emotional state in any situation?

In NLP, we have one simple word for any external stimulus that induces a change in our emotional state: we call it an "anchor." A state can be positive or negative; it can be excitement, depression, rage, joy, fear, and everything in between. That one song that makes you suddenly sad, the car that cuts you off and fills you with rage, the smell of Grandma's apple pie that makes you incredibly happy—they're all anchors!

This concept, which classical psychologists call "classical conditioning," started back in 1902. Dr. Edwin B. Twitmyer, a professor of Psychology at the University of Pennsylvania, was working with reflexes. He was the first to use a small rubber hammer to tap below a person's kneecap to induce the leg to jerk up. Before he tapped, though, he would warn the patient that he was about to tap. After he did this a few times, he noticed something peculiar—once the patient was used to it, their leg would go up before he even tapped them! He then wondered if he could associate something else with the reaction, so he began ringing a bell before he tapped. He would do this a few times, and then he would only ring the bell. And guess what? The subject responded with the reflex *only to the bell!* What's more, the patients *couldn't help it.* The reaction to the bell was so deeply unconscious that even when they tried, they couldn't keep their leg down! Twitmyer published this as his doctoral dissertation in 1902 and called it the "knee jerk reaction."

Unfortunately, no one paid much attention, because, just two years later, a Russian physiologist called Ivan Pavlov wrote a paper called the Conditioned Response after working with dogs and their digestion. You may have learned about Pavlov, who would show the dogs a certain meat paste, and the dogs would salivate. Soon, like Twitmyer, Pavlov learned that the dogs' salivary reflex started before they could see or smell the paste—it started on sight of the lab technician! So Pavlov started ringing a bell even before the technicians showed up, and—as we all can now guess—the dogs would salivate.

Since Pavlov, we've learned that humans' nervous systems work the same as those of dogs—an event that has nothing to do with a person's state will automatically link to that state if they occur at the same time.

In fact, any time something happens when we are in an intense emotional state, the two will be linked neurologically. And these anchors are strengthened by the intensity of the emotion, as well as the timing, uniqueness, and replication of the stimulus. But the most important idea is that the more often that same thing happens when you're in that same state, the stronger the anchor becomes!

Anchoring was taken to the next level by John Grinder and Richard Bandler in the 1970s. As they first developed NLP, Grinder and Bandler realized that anchors are basically a primal form of programming our brain. When someone "pushes your buttons," they're actually pushing your buttons! If you've ever been around NLP, or attended a seminar with me, one of my trainers, or even someone like Tony Robbins or Chris Howard, you've experienced anchoring, both overt and subliminal. The focus of NLP, however, was to take things that are done unconsciously all the time, and start to do them consciously.

So Grinder and Bandler started deciphering all the different ways anchors play a part in our lives, and discovered methods of creating new anchors on purpose. They then discovered ways to increase the power of these anchors, ways of putting certain anchors in order so each one induces the next, and even methods to completely obliterate the anchors we no longer want!

THERE'S THAT LOOK AGAIN

As I mentioned earlier, anchors can be stimulated by any one of the five modalities (visual, auditory, kinesthetic, olfactory, and gustatory). They're commonly associated with smells, but probably more prevalent (and more surreptitious) as visual, auditory, and kinesthetic stimuli. These stimuli occur all day, every day, and affect us in ways we never knew.

Imagine that every time you're tired or pissed off, a certain person always looks at you with the same concerned face. Soon, whenever you see that look, you get tired and pissed off. "What the hell do they mean with that look?" you might say. Or even, "Stop pitying me, and get out of my face!"

Now imagine that person is your spouse. It might cause problems, right? But this isn't their fault, and it's not your fault either. It's just a side effect of being human, of having a nervous system, and of not knowing how to use it.

When couples want to quit doing therapy and just have a complete breakthrough, anchoring is always a huge piece of the puzzle. Two people will come to me, completely unable to even look at each other, and they walk out after just a few hours like teenagers in love. You have to see it to believe it, but once you understand anchoring, anything is possible.

Here's what usually happens. When couples come in, I'll begin with a series of questions in order to discover what their old anchors are. Then I'll collapse (eliminate) the anchors they don't want, like frustration, stress, hurt, anger, etc. I just completely erase them! Then I help them install some new anchors, so that when one spouse looks at the other or says a certain thing, it triggers a *positive* emotional response, like the feelings that they used to get when they first started dating. This can literally resolve a decades-long problem in just a couple hours!

SO WHAT?

As a teenager, I smoked pot all day, every day. It wasn't the feeling that I became addicted to, or anchored to. It was the whole process, the whole ceremony that went on. Do you know what I'm talking about?

See, every time I thought about smoking pot, I would get a picture in my head that I was going to do it. As soon as I saw that picture, I would also get a feeling in my stomach, telling me *I just have to do this.* As soon as that feeling rose, I would find myself jumping up, going over to my desk where I had my stash, grabbing everything I needed, walking over to the window, hopping out, and going over to my special spot to get high. I'd go through this whole process every time, and I never once stopped to think about what I was doing. It was only in my adult years that I was able to look back with full awareness of what had been going on.

See, the first anchor (for me) was an external visual anchor. Whenever I saw a drug, or sometimes alcohol, it would fire off the anchor. At first, it carried with it a feeling of excitement, but by the end of my addiction, it had actually turned into a feeling of dread. Either way, I did the same thing. I just felt compelled to do it. As soon as I saw the stash, my feelings overwhelmed me.

Some of you reading this book have actually been addicted, and others have a loved one who has gone through addictions or alcoholism. For those of you who truly feel that you have an addiction to a certain stimulus—it can be alcohol, drugs, food, sex, shopping, or any other compulsion—it's important to find out which part of the process of addiction you're anchored to. Once you know that, you'll know exactly which of the upcoming techniques will help the most!

SPECIFIC TYPES OF ANCHORS

As I stated earlier, NLP has taught us all kinds of techniques that have to do with anchors. We can establish powerful anchors, which I call "Champion States." We can destroy old, negative anchors, a process called "Collapsing Anchors." Or we can string them together, with each anchor sparking the next, to drastically shift between states, in a process called "Chaining Anchors."

For all of these, we're going to create our own Kinesthetic stimulus. Since we're doing it on ourselves, we simply have to touch our knuckles or fingertips. Use whichever hand you want, and whichever fingertips, but make sure you use a different location for each exercise, so you don't cross-contaminate. Anchoring Excitement and Tranquility on the same place would get mighty confusing!

CHAMPION STATE

We set up anchors unconsciously throughout our lives; I believe it's time to set up some anchors that are truly helpful, and set them up on purpose! The first type of anchor is called a Champion State, because we use it to unleash our inner champions, that part of us that has total confidence and maximum impact.

Since this book is about addiction, let's begin with a Champion State specifically related to temptation. As we've discussed, an attachment to substances and behaviors becomes addictive when people begin to act out of a sense of compulsion rather than choice. A Champion State is a great tool that can be used to combat the compulsive element of this behavior.

Let's say you're going out tonight, and you don't want to drink. But when you get to the bar, and see people all around you drinking, you start to feel disempowered.

Maybe your friends are having a great time, and all of a sudden you just start to feel left out. Your friends seem to assume you should drink, but you aren't. It's confusing for them, and it's confusing for you. You made the decision not to drink, but it looks like fun...

At this point, what differentiates you from that person across the bar who's not drinking but still having a good time? Well, when that person was at home, he or she made an empowered decision, based on a powerful state that he or she was in at the time. Maybe that person was in a state of total confidence, and certain in their decision not to drink. In fact, the person may have been excited about the opportunity to find new ways to have fun! Already we have three different emotions he or she may have felt: *confident, certain,* and *excited.*

I'm sure you've felt these three emotions at some point in your past, too, even though it may not have had anything to do with alcohol or friends. One awesome aspect of the Champion State is the simple fact that it doesn't matter what context the emotions came from—they're just as powerful regardless of their source!

Are you ready to start? Great.

STEP 1: Now that you know what your disempowerment felt like, the first step is to define 3 states that you *would* like to feel instead. This is crucial; be clear on how you *want* to feel.

(I'm sure you're getting this by now, but I just want to be clear: your brain doesn't process negatives. Therefore, you can't anchor in a *not* state, like "*not* depressed" or "*not* powerless." If you anchored *not powerless*, your brain ignores the negative, and you'd just end up reinforcing that negative state that you wanted to avoid in the first place! If I were with you, I'd ask, "If you're not powerless, what *do* you feel?")

You might say simply, "I want to feel powerful." Or you might be more specific (since specificity produces better results) and, like that person across the bar, decide you want to feel *confident.* I can't tell you what you want to feel—it's different for everyone—so make sure that whatever emotions you choose works best for you.

Your three emotions can be whatever you need, but they should be similar to each other. They can be *proud, enthusiastic,* and *certain.* In other situations, they might be *playful, loving,* and *passionate,* or any other three that work well together.

For purposes of this exercise, I'm going to pretend that we're trying to be just like that person across the bar, feeling extremely *confident, resolute,* and *excited.*

STEP 2: In order to create a Champion State, we have to anchor each state separately, but *all in the same place.* The easiest thing, if you're going to do it on yourself, is to take your index finger and your thumb of one hand and squeeze them together. The act of squeezing those digits together becomes the trigger for that Champion State, so practice a few times and make sure you hit the exact same part of your finger each time. We actually "stack" the anchors on top of each other, so repeatability is extremely important!

(I actually have 8 separate Champion States, one on each finger! My right hand is my Empowering hand, and my left hand is my Calming hand. In my audio product called *Unleash Your Inner Champion*, I take you through the process of creating a Champion State just like you were there in front of me.)

Now that you have the emotions decided on, and a solid location you can repeatedly touch, we're ready to begin!

STEP 3: It's time to start anchoring. Let's start with *confidence*. Can you remember a time when you felt *totally confident?* Can you remember a specific time?

(If you really just can't think of a single time when you were totally confident, simply ask yourself, "Can you imagine a specific situation in which I *would* feel totally confident?" Or, if that doesn't work, can you think of a specific situation where somebody close to you felt totally confident? Just imagine yourself taking their place in that circumstance—remember Perceptual Positions?—and you're set to go. Personal memories produce the best results, but these other options work when they need to.)

Go back to that specific time and get Associated into the memory: look through your own eyes. See what you saw, hear what you heard, and really feel what you felt when you were *totally confident.*

Once you have that model in mind, whether it's your own experience, one you imagined, or someone else's, it's time to anchor the feeling. As you approach the peak of that state, squeeze your fingers together, then let go as the feeling reaches its maximum—before it starts to fade. Keep seeing what you saw, hearing what you heard, and feeling what you felt until the state floods through you once more; again, anchor as the feeling rises, and let go as it peaks. The feeling may rise and fall within you like waves on the ocean, so repeat this a few times, on the same finger, to really solidify it.

STEP 4: Now that you've anchored confidence, simply repeat Step 3 to add *certainty* to the same location. Remember a time when you knew everything was okay, and you felt certain you were doing the right thing and making the right decisions. Again, as the state rises within you, squeeze the same fingers together to stack onto the same anchor.

STEP 5: Repeat the anchoring once more, for the final state: *excitement.*

Once you've created this Champion State, you can use it whenever you feel powerless, guilty, upset, or any other negative state, and it will bail you out. The strength of an anchor subsides over time unless you recharge it, so make sure you take time to repeat this exercise every so often!

So Champion States are great for creating new anchors to get you out of a state you don't want to be in. But how do you avoid that negative state in the first place?

COLLAPSING ANCHORS

Now that we know how to stack and create a Champion State, it's going to be very easy to erase old anchors, in a process called "collapsing anchors." This process takes only about five minutes, but can change a lifetime of negative emotions!

In the same way as a visual stimulus led me to smoke marijuana, everyone has a "trigger" that leads to a compulsive behavior. It could be a place they go, or a particular person's face, a song they hear, etc.—anything could be a trigger, as long as when they were in the addictive state when they saw, heard or felt the stimulus.

So now imagine: you've been off sugar for 6 weeks. All is well. You are starting to feel better about life, losing some weight, and having more energy! Yes! But then you meet a friend at a coffee shop you used to go to every Sunday. You have no desire for sugary items right now, but then you walk into the shop…

The urge suddenly hits you! You just really have to have a mocha. And those donuts look delicious! Why? Maybe it's when you smell the smells, or when you see the rack of pastries, or when you hear the barista ask if you would like anything else, or maybe just walking through the door is enough to send you over the edge. Suddenly, you're feeling differently than you did before.

At this point, STOP! Take a breath, and realize that you're not backsliding, you're not weak, you're not losing it! All that is happening is that an old anchor from how you *used to feel* is being fired off. Rather than fighting it over & over, wouldn't it be so much easier to just delete that anchor? What if you felt no different when you smell, see, or hear that certain something? That is exactly what collapsing anchors is for—to erase an existing anchor.

STEP 1: The first thing we need to do is figure out exactly what we are negatively anchored to. In this example, maybe we realize it was the smell of the pastries that did us in. Whatever it is for you, figure out the exact moment you start feeling how you don't want to feel, and then figure out what sparked that in the first place. It's easier than you think, if you just close your eyes and go back through a specific memory step by step, stopping at the *moment* your state changes.

STEP 2: Next, decide on the location of your anchor. For this exercise, we need two different places, close to each other—I like to use two knuckles of my hand. Practice using two fingers to touch two knuckles, repeatedly in the same exact place.

STEP 3: Now, simply imagine that anchor happening. Go back to that specific memory, and slow down time as the anchor first happens. Associate into the memory, seeing what you saw, hearing what you heard, and (especially in this case) smelling what you smelled. How does it make you feel? What desires or negative emotions run through your body?

Just as in the previous exercise, we're going to anchor this state to one place. As the feelings rise up within you, touch one knuckle, and release as the feelings peak. If your state wasn't very strong that time, keep anchoring as the feeling rises until you have a solid sense of the feeling. Then stop. Think about your favorite movie for a moment to break your state.

STEP 4: Go through the Champion State exercise (above) and anchor three powerful emotions onto the *other* knuckle that you used in Step 2. In this example, you might want to use states like *decisive, empowered, centered, courageous,* etc. The feelings should be very intense, so pick states that are easy for you to access. Remember to repeat each state a few times, and then stack the others on the same knuckle! It's most important that this positive anchor is stronger than the negative anchor, so if you think it's not strong enough, simply stack additional positive states on top.

At this point, you should have one Negative state anchored on one knuckle, and at least three positive states anchored on the other. Now comes the fun part, the Collapse.

STEP 5: To collapse the negative anchor, fire off both triggers at the same time. Simply use your two fingers to press on each of the knuckles of the opposite hand at the same time. Hold them both like that for five seconds, then release only the negative anchor, holding the positive anchor for another 5 seconds or so.

This exercise may evoke a strong physiological reaction in you; if that happens, don't worry! I have plenty of students and clients whose faces start to twitch, whose bodies start to shake, and whose eyes even cross when they go through this, and then it all passes and they feel great again.

See, this process actually triggers your neurology to send two opposite neurological messages simultaneously. The result is two conflicting reactions spreading through your body for a few seconds. Finally, the stronger feeling (the stacked emotions) wins out, as if there was a tug of war in your brain.

This may result in a vivid reaction, or the whole process might feel very neutral, and you may even question whether it really worked. If this happens, it's a sign that it *did* work, and that you've truly incorporated the change! If nothing changed, you'd still be stuck in the negative emotion, wouldn't you?

To double-check this, you can wait a minute and press on your first knuckle again. If the process didn't work, this would have triggered the negative emotion. But if you were able to follow my directions, that negative emotion disappeared, right? Or did pressing the negative knuckle trigger the positive feelings instead?! Even better!

The real test is, of course, going back into the coffee shop. Go back to experience your trigger, and notice how different it feels, how the old state just isn't the same. Many people say it's as if they'd never even had the problem in the first place! You've regained your choices, and are one step closer to total freedom.

You can use Collapse Anchors for virtually any emotional state. It's not just for addictions!

CHAINING ANCHORS

The last type of anchoring, very useful for dealing with addictions, is called Chaining Anchors. Sometimes you find yourself stuck in a certain state or emotion, unable to get out. This stuck state might not have been triggered by any one stimulus, so we can't collapse it...what do we do?

Let's say you feel very stuck, in a state of self-doubt. This happens a lot to addicts, who feel powerless to change anything about their life.

There's a cliché about people who smoke marijuana, that they never get anything done. Let me tell you, from personal experience, it's not far from the truth! That super-lazy, procrastinating, immovable feeling, like you just don't want to do anything, seems like a natural side effect of almost any depressant, but it's all in your mind. After all, it's up to your brain how much hormones and neurotransmitters you get, isn't it?

Since that's just a problem of your imagination, the solution is in your imagination as well. But to go from being in that state of Procrastination to feeling totally Excited to move forward with something good (work, or a project, or spending time with loved ones) seems like a pretty big leap, right? On a scale of -10 to +10, persistent procrastination might be a -5 or so, and totally driven would be a +10!

In such cases, using a Champion State might not be effective enough by itself because procrastinating and being driven are so far apart from each other. In such cases, it's time to Chain Anchors!

This type of anchor is a bit more complex than the ones we've talked about previously, because it involves four (or more) anchors.

STEP 1: We have a Stuck State, the state of mind that we don't like, and an Action State, where you know you're going to do what you want to do. Now, we need to find two or three "Chain States" that fall between where you are and where you want to be, which will pull you toward your Action State. These should be states that are progressively more active than the first, but less active than the final state.

Let's go back to the example. If you were procrastinating, it's a logical next step to get to "Curious," right? Even when you're at your least active, I'm sure you've had glimpses of curiosity. It's not enough to make you do anything, but that's why it's a Chain State and not the Action State. It's maybe a 0 on the scale, pretty neutral.

The next state should be a bit higher than that. Maybe you'd call it "Intrigued." Maybe that's about a +5. If you're like me, you move easily from Curious to Intrigued.

Finally, you could move straight from Intrigued to Excited. +10.

STEP 2: So now we have a chain that goes from Procrastinating to Curious, to Intrigued, and finally to Excited. We'll use our knuckles to anchor these states, like in the last exercise, but this time each state gets its own knuckle. Get associated into a specific memory you have of being in each state, and anchor them individually to the four knuckles on your hand as you've been doing.

STEP 3: Firing these anchors is tricky. It's next to impossible to explain in a book, but live demonstrations make it simple. Basically, it's a process of firing off the first anchor, and as that feeling peaks, firing the next one. As the 2nd feeling peaks, you'd release the first anchor at the same time as you press the 3rd. Continue like this, never holding more than two anchors at a time, until your final Action State peaks within you. Release all the anchors at this peak, and feel the changes within you!

The results are amazing. You can test it by firing off the Stuck State anchor and feel as you go naturally through to the Action State, automatically!

Setting up a Chain of Anchors involves extremely precise and complex work, so don't get disheartened if it's not working exactly the way you'd hope. This is not something I would recommend you try on your own without at least seeing it done first. Come to one of our live courses to get more in-depth with anchoring, and you'll be surprised at how easy it can be!

ANCHORING EXTRAS

Remember, addictive behaviors involve certain rituals. Whether you're a smoker, a drug user, or engaged in any other addictive behavior, you tend to get into mini-rituals. These rituals may take only a few minutes, but they follow the same pattern every time. It's probably an unconscious pattern that we may not even recognize! But now, we have the tools to interrupt the pattern at the moment it is triggered, completely changing it forever.

Next time you see yourself about to do what you don't want to do, interrupt the pattern before you go on autopilot. Do something outrageous: jump up and down, yell something, or bark like a dog. It doesn't matter what you do; just pick something that is completely out of the ordinary to interrupt the mini-ritual.

Whenever we interrupt the unconscious mind from one of its patterns—things that it doesn't have to think about doing—it is becomes open to further instructions. Have you ever stepped off the curb you didn't realize was there? Have you walked up or down a flight of stairs and come to the end thinking there was another step? It feels weird, doesn't it? It isn't just that your legs are off-balance; it's that an unconscious pattern got interrupted.

In the same way, when you interrupt the pattern associated with an addiction mini-ritual, your mind will stop for a few seconds to await new instructions. In those few seconds, you can tell it, "I'm hungry. Maybe *I want salad*?" Or "that's right, I want to go for a walk."

In our NLP trainings, we spend a whole day teaching and practicing this art, called a "pattern interrupt." These very fast, simple tools can totally transform any negative pattern or ritual.

CHAPTER 16
IT'S ABOUT TIME

Have you ever been chastised for being late to a meeting, when you didn't think it was a big deal? Or maybe you get laughed at for being so anal about always being early for things. Who's right: the lazy people or the anal ones? Or, should I say, the easygoing people or the responsible ones?

As I'm sure you've learned by now, our minds are sort of like computer hard drives, which store every piece of information somewhere on a platter based on a series of ones and zeros. But we have a much more complex memory structure than computers do. Instead of ones and zeros in specific places in our brains, we store our memories as representations, containing all of our emotions, beliefs, decisions, memories, and identities. These representations, as we've discussed at length, come from the five senses, and are stored based on certain factors like location, motion, and intensity.

But we also store our memories in a more important, structured, predictable way: we use time. Every experience is stored in our minds not only spatially, but temporally as well. By temporally, I mean we store it in time, at a certain age in our memory. All of our memories can be found somewhere along our personal timeline.

Every one of us has a timeline, even if we're not aware of it. Let's do a simple exercise. As with most things in this book, this is an imaginative process, not a biochemical one. In answering the questions posed by this exercise, go with your first, gut-level response, not your intellect. This is important, because we need to know how your *unconscious* stores time, not your conscious brain. There are no right or wrong answers, no good or bad! All I ask is that you use your body to respond to the following questions—just doing it in your mind isn't good enough.

What's your first response when I ask, "Which direction is your past? Point toward the past." Again, don't think—just point.

Great! Now, where is the future? Point to the future, quick!

Awesome. And where's "Now?" Point to wherever the present moment is for you.

Got all three directions? Do you remember where you pointed? Excellent. Now notice how those three points form a sort of line? Maybe it's straight, maybe it's curvy, or maybe it's totally loopy; whatever it is, it's great.

There are infinite variations of timelines, just like fingerprints. But years of experience and study have taught me that there are two major ways most people tend to store their timeline.

Many people will point behind themselves for the past, directly down or even at their chests for now, and straight ahead of themselves for the future. These people see their timeline going from back to front.

Many other people will have pointed to the left for the past, straight down for now, and to the right for the future. These people see their timeline that way, from left to right.

Sometimes the angles in which people point are slightly different, or occasionally a left-handed person will store the past to the right and his or future to the left. That's fine. If you're comfortable with your timeline, you don't want to change it.

But, if it's not working for you, then that can cause lots of personal dilemmas. Maybe you're frustrated because you're constantly late for appointments, or maybe you get sick of always watching the clock!

Luckily, there is an incredibly easy way to change the way your timeline works! I'll discuss that later in this chapter, so stay tuned.

IN TIME

Like many people, my timeline passes from behind me, into my body, and out the front. When someone says, "You've got to put the past behind you," they are obviously the type of person who stores their timeline this way. Similarly, people who say they are "looking forward to the future," likely store time in this manner. This is what is called an "In-Time person."

An In-Time person, like it sounds, sees their body actually *in* the stream of time. It goes right through the middle of their body. In my case, for example, the Past is behind me, Now is right here in my chest, and the Future is in front of me. Thus, I'm right smack in the middle of it.

Because they are actually in the stream of time, In-Time people tend to live "in the moment." Whatever they're in the middle of is usually more important than what time it is, so they tend to think, "to hell with the schedule." They're nearly always 5, 10, or even 30 minutes late. Some entire cultures seem to be more In-Time than others: in the Middle East, for example, it's not at all uncommon to show up for a business appointment only to find the colleague you were supposed to meet is still talking to the person from two appointments before yours.

Whenever they finish with that person, they go on to the next one; when they finish the conversation with that person, that's when they meet with you. For In-Time people, it's rude to end a meeting on time if you're in the middle of a conversation!

For that reason, we often have "issues" with time management. We're often late for appointments or work, but we don't get upset about it. Other people, on the other hand, do get upset. These people tend to be Through-Time people. (We'll talk about them next.)

In-Time people also find it easier than others to move past things. If someone hurts you or doesn't agree with you, it's very easy to move on. Why? Because as soon as something occurs and becomes the past, it is, literally, behind you! Keeping a grudge is a tough act.

Last but not least, In-Time people generally find it easier than others to see their goals. (Whether or not they actually achieve them is a different matter.) Because their future is laid out in front of them, In-Time people see their goals naturally, and automatically stay focused on them. Since In-Time people like me move forward in their timeline, our goals start in the distance, then come up and smack us in the face!

THROUGH TIME

If you said your timeline runs from left to right (or right to left), you are a Through-Time person. This type of person can see the entire stream of time—past, present, and future—laid out in front of them. They can see Now just as easily as they see the Past or the Future. What does this mean?

Well, they deal quite differently with time than In-Time people do. Generally, these people are nearly always on time for appointments, if not five minutes early, because they're continuously aware of the entire stream of time; they see not only the present moment, but also five or ten minutes from now. This allows them to keep track of how much time is passing, and where they have to be. When in a meeting, they can see the time passing, and can imagine their next appointment getting upset, so they have little difficulty interrupting a meeting with someone to say, "Hey, I've enjoyed this conversation, but I do need to wrap it up; I need to be somewhere in ten minutes."

A simpler way to say this is that no time is more important for a Through-Time person than any other—the Past is as important as the Present Moment, which is just as important as the Future.

Unfortunately, this means that a Through-Time person has a hard time staying "in the moment," and literally cannot "put the past behind them." This sometimes makes it difficult for a Through-Time person to let go of the past. This is because they're always facing it! They're often sick of facing the past, but they can't avoid it.

ONE OF THESE THINGS IS NOT LIKE THE OTHER

Because of these inherent differences, In-Time and Through-Time people are often bumping heads.

In-Time people tend to look at Through-Time people as always rushing about, never taking time for their friends or loved ones. They feel that Through-Time people can't just be in the moment, and tend to think that they just don't "get it."

But how do you suppose Through-Time people look at In-Time people? They say, "Oh my God, they're always late and can't keep a commitment! Don't they respect my time?" They see In-Time people as though their head in the clouds, with no concept of time.

Each type of person believes that the other type is crazy! In fact, neither is crazy. It's just a difference in the way the two types process and store time.

I would encourage you to identify the timelines that everyone in your family uses. This is useful to know about your business partners as well, and everybody else who is important to you. Find out how they store time. You'll look at them a lot differently.

If you're a Through-Time person, and you find out that your husband or wife is an In-Time person, suddenly all the walls will drop. You'll see that what you once thought was disrespectful behavior and realize it was really just the product of how your partner unconsciously processes time. It has nothing to do with respect. It's just a different model of the world, in which they really, truly believe that it's "better" to be in the moment than watch the clock.

While this observation doesn't apply strictly to addictions, our perceptions of time do affect addictive behavior. Indeed, the development of therapy models around timelines has produced a radical way to eliminate the real root causes of addictions.

The whole field of Time Dynamics can be used to address the problem of secondary gains. Remember those? Perhaps there is a human need that is being met through the addiction or compulsive behavior, but that need really was created in a root-cause event. Often, some event in your life has created a string of emotions, beliefs, or decisions that have led to an addictive lifestyle.

In this case, Time Dynamics techniques are a way to eliminate the root cause from the past without having to regress into the past event. Simply put, Time Dynamics techniques are content-free! Someone who has been abused, molested, otherwise traumatized doesn't have to revisit the events and talk about them for hours (or even years) with a therapist. Some of my clients had talked to therapists for decades about the same problem or trauma, and they never made any progress!

Time Dynamics can address root-cause events in as little as 5 minutes. Yes, *it's that easy*. Moreover, these techniques absolutely eliminates the emotions related to the event, came from in the first place.

GESTALT STRINGS

If a behavior doesn't disappear after basic therapy, that's often because there is a root cause behind the behavior that basic therapy did not address. In such cases, we can use the concept of *gestalts* to address that cause.

Gestalt therapy looks at the events in your life like strings of pearls. Each pearl on the string is a certain event, emotion, or belief that develops over time. If you snip the very first pearl off, the rest just fall off automatically!

For example, let's consider the string of anger. Every time an event has led you to experience significant emotional anger, that event is like one pearl on the string. Some pearls are more significant than others, like the three or four times in the past when you really experienced strong and intense feelings of emotional outrage.

Traditional therapy latches onto those, and stops there. But if you continue to follow the string of events back to the beginning, you'll find they usually begin in your early childhood, *prior to the age of seven*. That first event is what we call the root-cause event.

Now, that particular event of anger may not have been significant and major, but it was the first time the person really experienced and acknowledged anger. This almost always happens as a very young child, probably before you even consciously remember.

Most people have an unconscious belief that if they let go of the emotion, then the event will cease to have any meaning. If that were true, then it would mean that they went through the horrible experience for nothing! But this couldn't be farther from the truth.

What we do in Time Dynamics is simply bring up that place on your timeline, without reliving the experience. We don't need to relive it. We simply go back on the timeline to the place where the memory is stored, and from that perspective, we can disrupt the memory and disconnect the emotion in a simple, effective, and permanent way. The event does not disappear, but the negative emotions attached to the event do!

EMOTIONS LINKED WITH LEARNINGS

When we go through a negative event, we often feel that we have learned something. Maybe we have "learned" that we always need to protect ourselves from love, or that we can't trust anybody. These "learnings" are stored as part of our timelines. We link the learning to the emotion of an experience at a certain point in time. This link—connecting the learning, the emotion and the experience—stays in position unless we do something to change it. The sad thing is that most people go through their lives with these unconscious linkages and never realize it.

Luckily, Time Dynamics allows us to replace such negative learnings with more positive ones. When we do this, it changes the memory's effect on our life (without changing the actual content) and frees us from the burdens of its negativity!

Time Dynamics is one of the most effective therapy models in existence today. These techniques address the emotions involved, without having to regress into the experiences. We're also able to use our Unconscious Minds to guide us to the right memory, instead of relying on our conscious minds, which often block or otherwise delete memories entirely.

We use Time Dynamics liberally in all of our courses, from weekends to advanced events, simply because it's so useful and can treat almost every personal issue without having to re-experience painful times in a person's life.

CHAPTER 17
FINAL THOUGHTS

In my personal journey, I've learned a lot from many different schools of thought that helped me further my personal growth and spiritual connection. This book is meant to foster understanding of why we do what we do and, in the process, give some answers about why no program is the only answer to addiction. However, they reflect what I have learned from years of studying psychology, self-improvement, 12-step programs, spiritual growth, and life's experience.

The information and exercises conveyed here are in no way obligatory, but I have used each and every one of them to help free clients from old beliefs, behavior patterns, and even addictions that are no longer serving them well.

When you finish reading this book, pass it on to someone who could use it. You would be surprised how things come to you at just the right times, and your friend may need it just when you give it.

Because of all that has happened to me, I'm glad I left home when I did. Even with all of the fear and not knowing, every day has worked out exactly as it was supposed to, hasn't it?

On that first birthday in my new apartment, I finally got to open my gift from a friend. It was a book. It was a book that had changed his life forever. He gave it to me, because he loved me that much. Maybe I enjoyed it so much, because I was so curious…

Things already started changing, that day I drove my new car home for the first time. I knew then that life would never be the same again. I knew that I had all the possibilities in the world in front of me, so I told myself, "You can do anything you wish to do."

And just like the characters in those old *Choose Your Own Adventure* books who always had a new choice coming at them, your answers to your own questions can always lead to something better. Whenever you start a new chapter, your whole situation changes!

Just like it did for me when I crossed the finish line of that marathon. It was surreal. Months of training, struggle, and pain all fell away in that one moment. I felt like I wanted to scream and cry and smile, all at the same time.

So I did.

And now it's time for your race. Go out there and win it

Download the *E-Book, FREE!*

Please help me share this message! **I am GIVING away the ebook!** If someone you know needs to read this book, Please share it with them now!

Give *Total Freedom From Addictions As an **E-Book** for **FREE!***

Go to:

www.addictedtonothing.com

Free DVD Valued at $97

In this brand-new DVD, Matt Brauning takes you through the **3 Keys to Unleash Ultimate Success**. Watch, and learn how to create the life of your dreams, and truly

MASTER YOUR LIFE

Order from the website to have the
Free DVD valued at $97 shipped to your home
Or watch online right now!

Order at:
www.AddictedToNothing.com

<u>Come See Matt LIVE!</u>

Join Matt for **his world-famous Success Revolution seminar!** In this *breakthrough weekend experience,* watch as life transforms before your eyes! Matt will take you through **creating the life you deserve now,** and help you **step into the future of your dreams!**

<u>*Receive up to* **2 FREE tickets**</u>
Value of $1590!

Transform your life today and reserve early.
Seating is extremely limited!

Read More and Register at:
<u>www.successrevolutionlive.com</u>

(Must register online to redeem your FREE tickets)